FORGOTTEN FASHION

FORGOTTEN FASHION

An Illustrated *faux* History of Outrageous
Trends and Their Untimely Demise

KATE HAHN

with illustrations by Andraé Gonzalo
of *Project Runway*

TOW
BOOKS

Cincinnati, Ohio
www.towbooks.com

For more fine books from F+W Publications, visit www.fwpublications.com.

12 11 10 09 08   5 4 3 2 1

Distributed in Canada by Fraser Direct, 100 Armstrong Avenue, Georgetown, Ontario, Canada L7G 5S4, Tel: (905) 877-4411. Distributed in the U.K. and Europe by David & Charles Brunel House, Newton Abbot, Devon, TQ12 4PU, England, Tel: (+44) 1626-323200, Fax: (+44) 1626-323319, E-mail: postmaster@davidandcharles.co.uk. Distributed in Australia by Capricorn Link, P.O. Box 704, Windsor, NSW 2756 Australia, Tel: (02) 4577-3555

Library of Congress Cataloging-in-Publication Data

Hahn, Kate, 1965-

  Forgotten fashion: an illustrated faux history of outrageous trends and their untimely demise / by Kate Hahn.

     p. cm.

  ISBN 978-1-58297-539-9 (pbk.)

  1. Fashion—Humor. 2. Clothing and dress—Humor. I. Title.

  PN6231.F36H34 2008

  818'.602—dc22

                                                        2008004516

Edited by Alice Pope
Designed by Claudean Wheeler
Art directed by Claudean Wheeler
Cover illustration by Andraé Gonzalo
Interior illustrations by Dena Blankmeyer, Teri Chung,
     Elizabeth Dran, Andraé Gonzalo, Amelia Haviland,
     Annie Lim, Lily Ng, Alison Petrie, Isabella Scotto
Production coordinated by Mark Griffin

F+W PUBLICATIONS, INC.

DEDICATION

To my smart and stylish grandmothers.

ACKNOWLEDGMENTS

I am indebted to the staff of the Beatrice P. Fruit Archives at the College of the Willows and to their assembled independent vetting team of fashion historians for allowing me unfettered access to the files of forgotten fashions. I am grateful to John Warner, Jane Friedman, Alice Pope, and Claudean Wheeler at TOW Books for their belief in and hard work on this book; and to our illustrators Andraé Gonzalo, Alison Petrie, Amelia Haviland, Annie Lim, Dena Blankmeyer, Elizabeth Dran, Isabella Scotto, Lily Ng, and Teri Chung. I am thankful to Taryn Fagerness; David Hochman for his encouragement; and above all Andrew Popp, for his years of love and support.

ABOUT THE AUTHOR

Kate Hahn has been a freelance journalist for seven years, focusing on beauty, fashion and entertainment. In addition to reporting, she writes personal essays and think pieces on trends. She has written about her ambivalence toward low-rise jeans guru Daniela Clark for Salon.com, and analyzed how men's hair trends reflect the mood of the country for National Public Radio's "Day to Day." Her writing has also appeared in *Newsweek, The Los Angeles Times,* and *McSweeney's.* She is a frequent contributor to *TV Guide,* and regularly covers shows that deal with fashion like *Ugly Betty* and *America's Next Top Model.* She has written over one hundred articles about beauty and style for a trade website called Behindthe Chair.com, which covers the salon industry.

TABLE OF CONTENTS

FORGOTTEN FASHION

An introduction

In your hands you hold a volume containing twenty-eight never-before-told tales of forgotten fashions from the early twentieth century to nearly the present day. These are the stories behind such formerly unsung sartorial concoctions as a Jazz Age flapper dress made entirely of ice; a mid-century French evening gown inspired by a refrigerator; a pair of Depression-era satin pajamas popularized by Hollywood with the help of an African elephant named Jinx; a 1980s suit made with gilded pinstripes; and the littlest little black dress, ever, along with many other creations that will surprise, shock, and delight you.

Sadly, each of the trends in this volume met an untimely, if not tragic, demise. They were the victims of a variety of misfortunes including bad weather, long wars, short tempers, wild animals, poorly formulated fabric blends, and even their creators, who include several Paris-trained couturiers, a Milanese tailor, a bourgeois Swiss teenager, and a man known only as "Hugo."

So, you may ask—you being of the curious and perhaps slightly suspicious temperament inherent to all good and wise readers of history—why are these forgotten fashions being remembered now? The occasion is the opening of a formerly secret fashion archive now stored at The College of the Willows, a private, two-year, postsecondary school for women, founded in 1849, in the tiny and genteel town of Riverbend, Virginia.

The archive was the personal collection of Willows alumna Beatrice P. Fruit (class of 1920). It includes press clippings, diary pages, letters, sketches, and ephemera. Miss Fruit's last will and testament stipulated that upon her death (which occurred in 2005) the collection be left to her alma mater, and the annals be opened for scholarly review. This volume makes available to the public just a small fraction of the archive that has so far been vetted by fashion historians.

"Bea," as she was known to her friends, was the ideal guardian of the records of forgotten fashions, and the reason for this is clearly linked to three facts about her life: Her family money came from the chain of Fruit Bros. department stores; she was an enthusiastic world traveler; and her father suffered from intermittent short-term memory loss and so was unable to recall many of his daughter's accomplishments. These factors shaped Bea into a woman who adored anything stylish, had a wide circle of international friends, and harbored a desire to preserve forever anything she sensed might be short-lived.

Because of the family business, she often traveled to the world's fashion capitals. Bea became known in design circles as the resolute rememberer of things others would rather forget, the keeper of fashion's unofficial history. If she did not observe and record a doomed trend firsthand, she often received in the mail a package from someone in possession of a debunked designer's portfolio or a stack of clippings about a must-have gone musty—a sender who knew Bea would make a better guardian of the heritage than they. Some of these offerings were so old, they had been stored away by their keepers when Ms. Fruit was still a child and as yet unknown as a conservator.

In this book, the forgotten fashions are arranged in chronological order, but you may view them any way you like. Each chapter is self-contained and never much more than a few pages long. Begin, perhaps, with your favorite decade and then work backward or forward. Skip randomly through titles or commence with the one that most intrigues. This book lends itself to casual perusal, much like a shopping trip along a crooked street of stores into which one can venture in and out on a whim, discovering in each a new collection of surprises.

SIDESADDLE MOTORING COAT

The great aunt of the trench coat, once removed

1903

Among the early automobiles tooling about the rutted lanes of Detroit, Michigan, was the Ladies' Ford Arabian, a luxury, single-seat electric motorcar. The vehicle came only in magnolia-flower white, was steered by an ivory-inlaid mahogany tiller, and had a buff-colored leather seat cut like a sidesaddle. A scant dozen were ever produced, all for a group of elite Detroit debutantes whose fathers were Ford investors.

To add distinction to the car, Ford included the Sidesaddle Motoring Coat with each vehicle and, as a courtesy, had it made to measure for each lady driver. The garment presented a more refined silhouette than the day's commonplace driving attire: the duster. Ankle-length, linen, and generous enough in cut to cover even the most ostentatious bustle, it was cinched at the waist with a belt of the same white patent leather that covered the Arabian's bumpers. Its wrist straps and shoulder cape have led some fashion historians to call it "the great aunt of the trench coat, once removed." The lucky girls could choose its color from a trio of pale pastels: pink, lilac, or green.

The designer, Dylan Graham, had refused to offer a fourth hue: eggshell. In his sketchbook, which he kept in lieu of a diary and which contains the only surviving drawings of the coat, he wrote, "To hell with Ford. The color implies too much fragility for a garment that will reach speeds of fifteen mph." Beside this is a fanciful drawing of an egg in road goggles, lying cracked beside smoldering auto wreckage.

Graham was a former British military officer who, before coming to the United States, had designed motoring dusters for both Aquascutum and Burberry ("A&B" as they were then known in the innermost outerwear circles). He hoped America would afford him the opportunity to start what he

ABOVE: View of the Sidesaddle Motoring Coat with shoulder cape and Quick Snap-Off System. From the sketchbook of designer Dylan Graham. Pencil, watercolor wash, 1903.

BELOW: Graham's doodle of a cracked egg in road goggles shows his preoccupation with safety. Pencil. 1903.

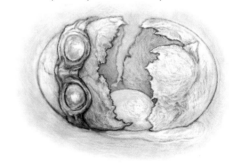

anticipated would be known as the "C" company. To aid in this alphabetically bolstered strategy for success, he named the coat the "Contego," Latin for "protect."

Graham was extremely safety conscious. He believed he had survived the Second Boer War thanks to his Burberry Tielocken military coat, the khaki color of which camouflaged him in the South African bush. With the Contego, his aim was to "defend against the enemies encountered whilst driving." It had a patented coated finish that resisted water, fire, dirt, and battery acid, and a trademarked Quick Snap-Off system that allowed the wearer to escape the garment in case a portion of it was pinned beneath the car in a turnover accident.

So concerned for safety was Graham that he insisted on accompanying Ford representatives to the gala garden party where they would personally deliver the Arabians. As Graham gave a demonstration of the Contego's safety features, one Holly Hollister remarked, "Mr. Graham, you must understand that we American girls are not made of fairy floss."

A reporter covering the event for the *Detroit Country Crier* recorded the exchange and noted that Graham seemed instantly smitten. The same paper was soon calling the girls The Steeplechase Suffragettes: "They race around the country lanes as if a loving cup were at stake."

The girls' parents, concerned at the increasing gossip about their daughters' overly independent and risky driving habits, and aware of Graham's commitment to safety, asked him to act as chaperone. Sailing along in a single-seat tonneau that had been quickly affixed to the back of Holly's Arabian, he studied firsthand how to modify the Contego to make it safer. His sketchbook drawings include reinforced lapels to repel the spray of road pebbles and hem spikes to ward off ankle-nipping dogs.

Yet the biggest danger was the girls themselves, whose smash-ups both Graham and the *Country Crier* recorded. Miss Jo Elby sideswiped an elm tree. Celia Nash meandered into a creek. Although none were hurt, their cars were totaled, and not replaced. Soon the merry outings were reduced to Graham and Holly. The sketches of safety features disappeared, replaced by Holly picking apples, Holly lying in the grass reading a novel, Holly in only a loosened corset and jodhpurs.

Then, in Graham's hand, the words: "Why did I invent nothing to safely protect my own heart?" Below this, there is a drawing of a cracked heart, in road goggles, lying in a dirt lane as an Arabian motors off into the distance. After this, there are only blank pages.

This abrupt ending is explained by two articles that appeared at about the same time in the *Country Crier*. First, Ford announced its future cars for women would not be open-air, but enclosed, making the Contego obsolete, and thus losing Graham his job and foothold in the U.S. market for the "C" company. The second was an engagement announcement for Holly Hollister to one Edward Christmas, CPA. British military records show that Graham re-enlisted and spent the balance of his life as one of the early champions of the new fabric that would prove so effective and save so many lives in World War II: camouflage cloth.

ABOVE: "Testing the suspension." Ladies Ford Arabian sidesaddle electric motorcar in action. From the sketchbook of Dylan Graham. Pencil. 1903.

BODY MUFF

A plantain conquers polite society

OPPOSITE: Illustration of a Body Muff in evergreen velvet with mink trim, from *Smith's Souk*, a short-lived periodical modeled after *Harper's Bazaar*. December 1905. The narrow ankle closure kept out winter drafts but made ice skating risky.

The winter of 1905 brought the usual freezing temperatures to the island of Manhattan, along with a flu epidemic that was soon dubbed the "Gilded Germ" because, as socialite and wit Harriet Wellington remarked, "Unlike the silver, it never goes home with the help." The outbreak infected only the upper classes, moving from ballroom to ballroom, causing some to speculate it was borne on the breezes of the waltz. To ward off the drafts believed to ferry the disease, stylish women adopted a new sort of gown for evening: the Body Muff, a full-length, fur-lined velvet cylinder, cinched at the neck and hem, where it was trimmed with ermine, fox or mink.

The Body Muff preceded French fashion designer Paul Poiret's famous narrow hobble skirt by five years, but the restrictive closure at the feet made walking just as difficult. It had a marked effect on women's gaits. According to Harriet Wellington, "The Fifth Avenue ballrooms are filled with what look like locomoting upright mermaids. Or, more accurately, mer-matrons."

The design was first worn by its creator Kitty Van Bleuve, an arriviste whose husband Heinrich had made a fortune in Honduran bananas. Relieved to escape the plantation and hoping never to return to the Caribbean coast, Kitty was intent on making her mark in New York. She feared that her years in equatorial climes made her especially vulnerable to contracting the Gilded Germ, which, although not fatal, could put her to bed for a month, thus killing her chances at entering society that year.

Much of what we know about Kitty's motivations, and the design of the Body Muff, comes from the diaries of her dressmaker, Mary. "Said to Miss, looks like a velvet banana skin, your dress. It did. All tight at the neck and ankles. The look she give me. Miss hates plantains. Even hates her own yellow hair, which makes angels jealous, just because of it reminds her of 'em."

It was Kitty's good luck to debut the Body Muff at a Central Park skating party, where her natural grace was showcased even in the slim confines of the gown. Her innate physical equilibrium had been perfected while pacing the deck during her many sea voyages with Heinrich, or striding up and down the plantation veranda on lonely nights, her gait wobbly from gin, gazing at the palm trees lining the drive for, what Mary reported she called, "vertical inspiration."

Kitty's rosy cheeks, blonde curls, and Persian blue velvet Body Muff made her the picture of health and vigor. After her debut at the skating party, her calling card tray overflowed. Socialites begged to borrow Mary, who grew so in demand that she ended up giving group lessons to other personal dressmakers. "Scissors near froze shut in the Astor attic. So cold. Way Miss rents me out," Mary wrote. Despite her resentment, the opera lobbies were soon crowded with velvet Body Muffs, in burgundy and gold moiré edged in striking silver fox or deep evergreen trimmed in mink.

Waltzing in the gowns was difficult, and although ice skating in them was not much easier, pond-top parties became all the rage, mostly because women wanted to emulate Kitty's graceful stroke, which became known as "The Van Bleuve Glide." Heinrich began a side business supplying flat panels of ice to those who wanted to practice the Glide in their gardens or ballrooms. The winter was prosperous and happy. Kitty was ecstatic. But toward the end of the season, Heinrich announced that in summer they would be returning to Honduras. "Maybe was this news made Miss take such a risk," Mary wrote, in a hand that had grown more ragged, probably due to arthritis caused by overuse of scissors.

During an afternoon skating party, Manhattan was pummeled by an unusually intense and warm rain, thought by today's meteorologists to be caused by the first mass deforestation efforts as Heinrich and his fruit cartel cleared trees to make way for more banana plantations. The deluge pounded the skating pond with the concentrated pressure of water moving through a fire hose. Kitty and her followers were instantly drenched. The weight of the rain-soaked velvet Body Muffs tripled, causing menacing long cracks to form in the ice. The others skated to safety, but Kitty refused to leave the pond. She fell through the ice and was dragged underwater by her gown. Even though there were valiant efforts by a nearby organ-grinder and his monkey, Kitty is thought to have drowned. Her body was never recovered. "Dress was her coffin," Mary wrote.

Heinrich returned to the banana plantation alone and, by all accounts, devastated. The pond was filled in and upon it constructed a granite memorial to Kitty. Mary left a banana there every day on the birthday of her former mistress, until she herself died in 1941. "Gave her a fortune, that fruit. Best thing to remember her by." The memorial was removed in the late 1980s when a group of Columbia University Latin American Studies students protested the use of public land to honor a colonialist.

TICKER TAPE TRIM

Paper ribbons and covert communiqués

In the early 1900s, a well-dressed woman was never without at least one item of clothing bedecked with ribbon trim. The satin strands might ornament underclothes (camisoles, drawers, and corsets), adorn daywear (white silk batiste lace tea gowns), or, according to a 1906 pamphlet from the short-lived organization known as The Movement for Night Dress Reform, "festoon sleepwear with such loud declarations of style that a lady is kept awake by her own finery, and arises without the requisite energy to contribute to the betterment of society."

But for some, ribbon was neither a must-have stylish detail nor a scapegoat for social ills. For this group of wealthy teenage girls, it was a means of secret communication—in the form of Ticker Tape Trim, ribbon made from the thin paper strands that emerged from the ticker tape machines kept at home by their fathers, who were stockbrokers and bankers. The paper adornments did not bear the stock quotes that arrived on the devices during the day, but messages from the girls' beaus, transmitted late at night by a moonlighting employee of the New York Stock Quotation company, who worked in an office above the trading floor.

The covert communiqués were retrieved by the girls after their parents had gone to bed. The messages were then woven into place in the position once occupied by the original ribbon trim, most often into sleeve-ends so they could be read repeatedly. This allowed a girl to sit on a prim Victorian settee or a hard schoolroom bench and dilute the scolding voice of a parent or teacher by running her eyes over the words of her beloved. The practice could be considered the twentieth century's earliest known form of "texting" between teens—the difference from today's

ABOVE: Most Ticker Tape Trim wearers were young women under the age of eighteen. A contemporary artist's rendering shows how the trim was used in place of ribbon in a corset neckline.

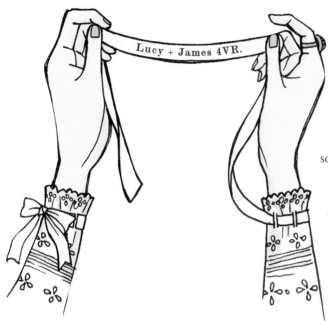

ABOVE: Declarations of love were usually the purpose of the communiqués.

OPPOSITE: A girl steals a rare private moment to reread the clandestine message woven into the cuff of her tea gown.

missives being that these were one-sided, with the girls unable to answer.

Surely the Panic of 1907, which caused not one but two stock market crashes that year, was a contributing factor to the trend, as more and more rich patriarchs installed ticker tape machines at home so as to have their eyes on the market at all times.

Excerpts of messages from the few surviving strands of Ticker Tape Trim include "Lucy+James 4VR. Lucy+James 4VR," printed on a three-yard length of trim woven into a corset neckline. "Oak Tree. 12AM. Elope. YOU 5k@9 ½," worked into the hem of a night dress (the inclusion of the partial stock market quote is a mystery). "Soul meets soul on lovers' lips. Recite Shelley with me again darling," wound about the sleeve of a tea gown and proudly tied into two pert bows. "23 skidoo Henry. He's Joe Zilsch. Forget him," folded, unused, in a box of old party invitations and greeting cards.

But our best source of information on Ticker Tape Trim comes not from the often-crumbling surviving examples, but from a letter to her sister written by Lily Williams, a young visitor to the temporary Venice, Italy, studio of the American painter John Singer Sargent, best known as a portraitist who documented the images of his country's elite. A lengthy passage is reproduced here.

"One of the most interesting canvasses in Mr. Sargent's studio remains unfinished. I found it only because I am wont to explore the dark corners of rooms, and this happened to be where it was standing. The great man rather hesitantly told me (he struggles with words) that the work is entitled, 'Reading the Ticker, the Daughters of Harold Blake.' Upon hearing that, I felt silly for not having recognized all four of the girls right away. You know them: Jane, Emily, Charlotte, and unfortunate little Betsey, who has that funny foot. I was quite surprised they allowed themselves to be painted while engaged in such a clandestine (for good reason!) and immoral activity—of which I have heard but never participated. But Jane likes to get attention, even if she must resort to shocking other people, so perhaps I see her motive. And since Mr. Sargent is no longer taking commissions, a fact upon which I sadly discovered him to be immovable, this may have been the only way she could have her visage preserved by his brush.

"At any rate, Mr. Sargent placed the painting against the wall. It is a large square, perhaps 90 × 90 inches. The scene is Mr. Blake's study in the Boston house—you are familiar with it from the time father sent you in on a dare at Christmas to steal cigars. The only light comes from a candelabrum, held aloft by Emily. Her finger is to her lips, and she glances nervously toward the door. You have surely seen her in this pose as Jane often makes her keep watch when the Blake sisters are up to something wicked. In the center of the scene is a wooden column atop which rests a bell jar that surrounds a cast-iron ticker tape machine, with a wheel spinning out the tape. I must say the skill with which Mr. Sargent has captured the candlelight on the glass dome is astounding, as is his depiction of the ostentatious detail of all the girls' French lace nightdresses—you know the Blakes. They must outdo everyone, even in the dark.

"With one hand, Jane holds a strand of tape as it emerges from the machine. With her other she extends more of the tape toward Betsey, who sits on that lovely Oriental rug, her poor little *pied* partially tucked underneath her as if to hide it, although Sargent has rendered the crookedness perfectly. Charlotte extends her sleeve, and Betsey weaves the tape into it. I was speechless, and I believe Mr. Sargent thought it was due to his talent with likeness. Of course it was, but I wondered who had sent Charlotte the message, and if the reason the painting was unfinished was that the Blake parents had decided against preserving their daughters' images for all eternity engaged in the practice of ticker tape trimming. It sullies them so! It seems odd to say that an image of a practice so vile is lovely, but it is. There are Sargent's beautiful darks and lights and free, energetic brushstrokes. Although, I daresay, the great man does exaggerate the thickness and curliness of the Blakes' auburn hair."

Here the relevant description ends, and the rest of the letter is concerned with a catalog of social visits. Although the account is quite vivid, art historians doubt the existence of the painting, as Lily Williams was well known in her time as a

gossip and spreader of sometimes socially debilitating rumors. But even if Williams is inventing a scene based on her own activities or those she observed elsewhere, and attributing it to the Blake girls in an attempt to ruin their reputations, as has been suggested, she does history a favor by revealing the social attitude toward ticker tape trimming.

Beyond the Williams missive, there are no other descriptions of the practice. The Blake girls did not keep journals, and little was written about their lives beyond what was recorded in the social register. Betsey is mentioned in a 1930 edition of the *American Journal of Podiatry*, in an article describing her successful operation to cure "tangled tendon" syndrome. Yellowed versions of Ticker Tape Trim continue to turn up in attics, pressed into diaries or mounted in scrapbooks, a tribute to the determination young people feel to create a language of their own.

PACING TROUSER

The ideal furnishing for the gentleman holiday-maker

These pajama-like drawstring trousers were originally intended as vacation wear for middle-class Englishmen, for whom, at the beginning of the twentieth century, the concept of "leisure" time was still a novelty. Sold exclusively at seaside resort hotels catering to families on the new "package holidays," the garments were developed by the London-based Holiday Trouser Company Ltd. (HTC Ltd.). They were made of linen-like material derived from an Indian Ocean seaweed species thought to promote health and well-being, and their capacious proportions and large slash pockets were intended to facilitate pursuits such as sand-castle building, tide-pool wading, and seashell collecting.

In a brochure, the cover of which shows a kite-flying man clad in the billowing *pantalon*, HTC Ltd. calls their product "The ideal furnishing for the gentlemen holiday-maker."

Yet the vacationing husband and father, impatient with the enforced "weekend" or "time out," found that the wide legs and generous cut were better suited to accommodate his long strides as he marched vigorously up and down the freshly laid wooden boardwalk in beach cities like Bournemouth—strategizing ways to mop the floor with his adversaries when he returned to the office. Thus the name "Pacers."

In the summer of 1910, many marine promenades were crowded with men clothed in the oatmeal-colored fabric, which was lightweight and flapped about easily in the stiff ocean breezes. We get a particularly clear image of the Pacer thanks to messages on the backs of a batch of picture postcards unearthed behind a wall adjacent to a mail slot at the now-demolished Seahorse Hotel in Penzance, all dated July 1910.

"The children and I sit on the beach while Simon plods in his Pacers with the other men. It is like watching the impatient

ABOVE: Illustration for the cover of the Holiday Trouser Company, Ltd. promotional brochure. 1910.

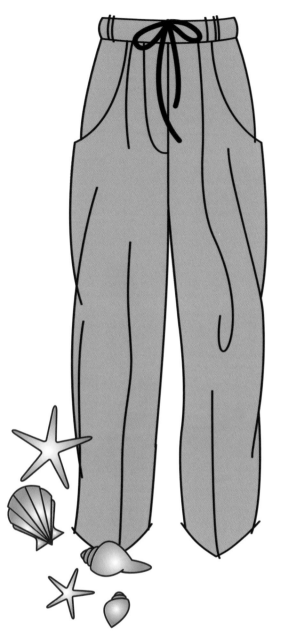

ABOVE: A drawstring closure and generous proportions were supposed to promote relaxation.

crowds on a tube platform—but the train never arrives. From our vantage point beside the surf, we play a new game: Which one is Daddy?"—Caroline Grant

"Father and his ilk stride all day, their Pacers blowing in the breeze. It is as if they are putting up sartorial sails, hoping to catch the currents that will ferry them to great wealth."—Rebecca Fox

"At sunset, it is difficult to pick out my own dear David from the row of men who stand facing the horizon. I guess I am really a married woman now!"—Mary Harvey

"We return to London tomorrow. I shall be relieved to leave our seaside paradise behind. George recently berated the children for building sand castles that lack modern amenities! He misses his estate business so."—Elspeth Summers

When brought home from the beach, the Pacer continued to disappoint, as it tended to molder. Some theorized that the seaweed from which the fibers of the cloth were made did not thrive inland. The men, careful with every line of the family budget, found the Pacer to be a bad buy, a cheap trick, a poor investment akin to cut flowers, and by the beginning of September, many had written letters to HTC Ltd. and the editors of their local papers to say so.

Epistles appearing in the *Leeds Daily* complain bitterly of the price, lack of measurable health benefits, and a distinct smell of must emanating from the fabric after a few days away from the sea, no matter how long and often the trousers were aired out. There was even a humorous poem, "Regrets on a Summer Purchase," by one Benjamin Knight Smith. One stanza reads:

Trousers sans creases: approach with trepidity.
Like a brow without furrows, they're born of stupidity.
The man who designed,
These string-fastened novelties,
Had a knot or two,
In his mental facilities.

HTC Ltd. sent coupons for replacement trousers to all of their dissatisfied customers, some of who remarked that this was like being offered a rotten tooth in place of one that had just fallen out.

Eventually a housewife named Sophie Simon, whose husband demanded she find a new use for the trousers without throwing them away, tried laying them over the flowerbeds in her back garden to insulate the tiny sprouts from the cold. As the Pacers disintegrated, they nurtured the seedlings, and, like some sort of miracle fertilizer, produced the hardiest and most colorful poppies Sophie had seen in years. She submitted the tip to a syndicated gardening column, and hundreds of women wrote to its author saying the method had worked similar wonders for both their annuals and perennials.

The following summer, avid horticulture hobbyists flocked to the beach resort hotel shops in search of the trousers. But the discovery of their secret benefits had come too late. The garments were no longer in production, as sales had plummeted due to their faltering reputation.

When HTC Ltd. liquidated, they took the remaining bolts of uncut seaweed health cloth and deposited them at a dump in rural England. Weeks later, the gentle hills of the trash repository bloomed with the most vibrant display of wildflowers ever seen in that part of the country. Looking out across them, one man was heard to remark that if only there was a way to patent the view and charge others to share it—now that would be something.

Most of the records of the Holiday Trouser Company Ltd. have been lost, having burned in a storage facility during the Blitz.

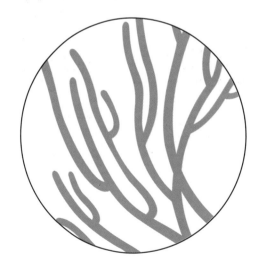

ABOVE: The species of seaweed used to create the fabric is not known.

PICASSO PATCHWORK

A dress declares war on Switzerland

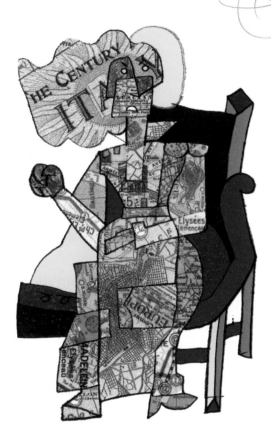

ABOVE: Cubist-inspired depiction of teenage designer Aiana Lilienstein in one of her Picasso Patchwork gowns. Collage. Attributed to her governess, Birgit. 1916.

"The sight of this latest fashion is a nightmarish hallucination that forces the average Swiss citizen to experience the world through the eyes of an absinthe drinker." "Hideous! These gowns should be locked up in wardrobes and never allowed out." "A bigger threat to our country than Germany!" These statements are excerpts from letters to the editor published in the summer of 1916 on the editorial pages of *Neue Zürcher Zeitung*, the daily paper of Switzerland's largest city, regarding one of the earliest examples of "street" fashion: a dress style called Picasso Patchwork.

The rebellious garment that inspired passions nearly as strong as those that drove the Great War raging beyond the neutral country's borders was the invention of sixteen-year-old Aiana Lilienstein, an angry only child distinguished by her perpetually tangled blonde hair and equally unkempt temper, who lived with her wealthy parents in an elaborate chalet on the shores of Lake Zurich.

Like the wavering reflection of the Lilienstein home in the blue water, a Picasso Patchwork gown gave the illusion of familiar solidity, until one noticed its ripples. At a distance, it bore the same silhouette as other ladies' fashions of the day: a raglan-sleeved bodice, nipped at the waist with a belt, finished with a full, calf-length skirt. Yet closer inspection revealed strange details—for the frocks had been neatly disassembled by Aiana upon receipt from her dressmaker and put back together again in a manner designed to shock.

A sleeve was snipped off and sewn onto the front of the skirt. In its place, a section of satin collar was used to create a new arm covering. A fresh collar was fashioned from a scrap of linen cut from the skirt. Front buttons were re-sited on the shoulders. A belt was worn backwards, the glint of the buckle matching that in Aiana's eye.

The reason for Aiana's sartorial mischief is made clear in reports her governess, Birgit, provided to Frau Lilienstein, who, as a popular hostess, had little time to spend with her daughter. "Aiana is copying Cubist painter Pablo Picasso, who depicts subjects in a fragmented manner. She believes the world is forever ripped apart and rearranged by the war and is trying to remind people of it. In a separate matter, the snarls in her tresses have broken another hairbrush, which she threw across the nursery, hitting a map of Europe that I had pinned to the wall, tearing it. I will need money to replace both."

Birgit was an amateur collagist, and some of the only extant images of Picasso Patchwork come from her paper assemblage portraits of Aiana, one of which contains scraps from the aforementioned map.

On frequent shopping trips to buy the household items destroyed during Aiana's fits of rage, Birgit took the girl with her to the Bahnhofstrasse, Zurich's main shopping street. But upon seeing Aiana's outrageous attire, merchants banned her from entering their stores. As she waited outside in the *strasse*, or street, day after day, her unusual garb was noticed by other bored and restless young girls in the Swiss bourgeoisie. Birgit wrote to Frau Lilienstein: "Young women are fascinated by Aiana's attire, more so when they see it provokes their mothers' distaste."

The quick rise in popularity of this "street" look is evident in an editorial in *Neue Zürcher Zeitung*: "This paper supports the city government's proposed ban on this style. Our tidy parks, clean promenades, and spotless squares are sullied by chaotically clad girls, their hair arranged in a puzzling array of Gordian knots." This passage makes it clear that Aiana's signature platinum tangles were copied, too.

The growing Picasso Patchwork trend excited girls to create increasingly elaborate and shocking versions of the style. Rivalries bloomed as each tried to top the next, a sort of battle that was not the result Aiana had intended. Birgit wrote to Frau Lilienstein: "You may have noticed from the broken crockery that Aiana is disappointed in her peers, who seem more concerned with the quality and arrangement of

ABOVE: Before and after. A contemporary artist's interpretation of the transformation of a typical 1916 gown to a Picasso Patchwork design. Note the accompanying fractured hairstyle.

georgette than the lives of our brothers across Europe. I will need some francs for a new soup tureen."

The receipt for the tureen can be seen in another of Birgit's collages, in which she depicts herself and Aiana at the Cabaret Voltaire, an avant-garde nightclub where dancers, musicians, and spoken-word artists from across Europe raged against the Great War. We can guess that Birgit brought her young charge here in a desperate attempt to end her tantrums by introducing her to a like-minded group. We can also assume it was here Aiana learned about more radical forms of artistic expression, such as Dada, a nihilistic art movement that found most creative endeavors pointless.

This would explain why, in late August, she staged a performance art piece on the Bahnhofstrasse, ripping her Picasso Patchwork dresses into long strips while shouting that she would donate them as bandages to a war hospital in France. Other girls soon followed suit (although they held gown-tearing parties in parlors, pastries were served, and the shreds tossed in the trash afterward), and the city fathers abandoned their campaign to criminalize the dresses.

NZZ wrote: "Rubbish bins overflow with colorful piles of what was once the most stylish sort of gown a girl could wear. It is the clearest illustration one will ever see of the fickleness of fashion." The paper makes note of Aiana one more time. After the war, in the 1920s, she is listed as one of the first women in Zurich to bob her hair. She later went on to drive ambulances in World War II and died at age seventy-two in a pacifist commune in France.

ROBE DE CHAMPAGNE

A mysteriously intoxicating bridal gown

A Parisian concoction often worn by French war brides for their weddings to American soldiers, the Robe de Champagne, or Champagne Dress, was a simple, loose-fitting, ankle-length chemise constructed of three layers of golden mousseline de soie, a fine, sheer, muslin-like silk. The silhouette was the boxy one so popular in the 1920s, but the luxurious, lightweight fabric gave the gown a floaty, frothy quality. That, and the fact that it was frequently donned for celebratory occasions, earned it the bubbly moniker.

Perhaps the most remarkable thing about the Robe de Champagne was that it was sold already embedded with perfume. This particular scent was available nowhere but on the Robe and was said to intoxicate the wearer with joy. The exact formula was unknown, but those who tried to guess at the recipe postulated a list of ingredients as widely varying as sandalwood, cognac, almond, and rose along with impossibly untraditional ones such as baked bread. The fragrance was so lovely that it rendered a bridal bouquet unnecessary, making the gown rather unpopular with florists.

The designer/perfumer was an American GI named Stumpy Schroeder, who had worked as a U.S. Army medic in World War I and become well regarded on the battlefield for his lifesaving snug tourniquets, nonscarring stitches, and remarkably effective array of homemade smelling salts. Before being drafted, Stumpy had studied at technical college to be an operator of industrial sewing machines and sold perfume at the Daniels & Fisher department store in his hometown of Denver. After the war, he remained in Paris, quietly paying employees of French couture houses to teach him their art in the evenings. When not sewing or designing, he studied

ABOVE: Robe de Champagne from the sketchbook of Stumpy Schroeder done in the style of illustrations typical of the French fashion magazine, *Gazette du bon ton*. Ink. 1923.

French fashion magazines such as *Gazette du Bon Ton* and *Art-Goût-Beauté* in his small garret room.

Stumpy's idol was Jeanne Lanvin, the couture designer and founder of the first Paris fashion house, who made not only clothes but menswear, home décor, and perfumes. He modeled himself after Lanvin, haunting her elegant shop on the rue du Faubourg Saint-Honoré. Where Lanvin's signature color was a forget-me-not blue, Stumpy chose a champagne hue. Where Lanvin's logo was a golden image of herself and her daughter, Stumpy's was a silver one that depicted him and his dog, a three-legged greyhound named Claude that he had found wandering in the Tuileries gardens and nursed back to health.

Although Stumpy did not originally intend his Robe de Champagne as a wedding gown, it grew popular as such by word of mouth. Many of the soldiers he had tenderly stitched up on the battlefield remained in French hospitals for months after the war was over. Doctors remarked that it was a miracle they had survived at all, and attributed it to Stumpy's skill. Some of the wounded men said it was Stumpy's smelling salts that had made them want to live, reminding them of the things they loved about the world even as they lay in pain on the battlefield.

These men often proposed marriage to their nurses, physical therapists, or the girls who came around to water the plants on the hospital windowsills. The weddings occurred shortly after the question was popped, as the soldiers had to return home. But there was the problem of what the young woman should wear at the ceremony. When the vets found out that Stumpy was making dresses, they insisted their fiancées try them on. They told their friends and word spread across the wards.

The girls visited Stumpy for fittings in his narrow shop—little more than a glorified former walkway, roofed by a greedy landlord and located between a boucherie and a patisserie. The fit of the dresses was so universally flattering, the scent so intoxicating, the new love for their North American husbands so intense, that none of the customers seemed to care that the gown she wore on the most important day of her life would be identical to that of one or more other brides.

ABOVE: Symbol of the House of Schroeder, depicting the designer and his three-legged greyhound, Claude. Note the similarity to the Jeanne Lanvin logo. Silver leaf. 1923.

Stumpy often went to see off his newlywed couples at the docks for their journeys home. He taught Claude to wave good-bye as well, and the two became a familiar sight among the bon voyage streamers.

Once back in Sacramento or Kansas City, many of the men whose lives Stumpy had saved on the battlefield wrote to say he had done it a second time over on the home front. A typical missive reads: "Sophie cries for Paris, but then she goes to the closet and buries her face in that Champagne dress you made, and in fifteen minutes she's back to making meatloaf. Thanks Stump!"

Although Stumpy's dresses were popular and, as the above excerpt suggests, remained beloved long after the wedding day, the eventual exodus of most American vets from Paris cut into his business. He could no longer maintain his small shop, pay for the fine fabrics he preferred, or care adequately for Claude, who suffered back problems. Stumpy eventually went to work for Lanvin and is said to be one of the uncredited "noses" that helped design her famous Arpège perfume. And the mysterious scent of the Robe de Champagne? Some have guessed that, somehow, Stumpy had managed to distill Paris itself.

ABOVE: The formula for the perfume embedded in the fabric of the Robe de Champagne was never made public, but the aromas were reported to be as wide-ranging as sandalwood, cognac, almond, rose and freshly baked bread.

1927

The ultimate in planned obsolescence

In the late 1920s, beaded evening dresses had become so popular in the United States that a French exporter of the gowns remarked, "The American hunger for the new is insatiable. A dress one hour old is stale. One purchased a month before is rancid. These savages' intolerance for the old will bankrupt them."

One of these "savages" was Miss Isabella Grant of Cincinnati, Ohio, heiress to the fortune of Grant Frozen Novelties, a company that had made millions peddling dessert products that capitalized on current events. In the summer of 1927, their biggest seller was a four-inch-long vanilla ice cream replica of Lindbergh's *Spirit of St. Louis* airplane, speared on a wooden stick. Izzy equated embracing the "new" with getting rich, so she bought the very latest fashions without fear of financial ruin.

With her brunette Eton crop and flapper style, she epitomized the era's "It Girl," and was often featured in the company's illustrated magazine advertisements, decked out in the latest wonder of Parisian beadwork. In a July 1927 picture, she stands licking a "Lindy" beside a sparkling swimming pool, wearing a sleeveless, aqua-colored, drop-waist beaded shift that bears an art nouveau pattern of stylized waves.

Yet Miss Grant longed to be more than an image on a page. She wanted to prove she had the same capitalist moxie as her mother, who had died tragically of heat exhaustion after pushing an ice cream cart for twelve hours straight when Izzy and the family business were both only two years old. Upon visiting her father's factory one day, Izzy hit on the idea for a new frozen novelty, one that would make her reputation as a businesswoman: a beaded dress made entirely of ice.

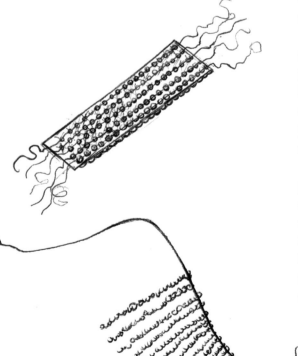

BELOW: Wooden molds used to make ice beads. Pencil sketch found in the margins of the Grant Frozen Novelty Company's accounting ledgers. 1927.

Mr. Grant put his finest artisans (who had designed the forms for the "Lindy" pop) at his daughter's disposal. Under her direction, they created "ice beads." These began as pure mountain spring water trucked in from the Grants' country estate, and were incubated in custom molds with intricately faceted interior surfaces. Once hardened, they had the glitter of finely cut gems. Food coloring was added to different batches to create a wide palette of shades.

Each frozen bead was pierced through with a heated needle. Some were then strung onto sturdy lengths of thread, which were assembled to form the tiers of fringe that make up the familiar flapper dress. Others were sewn individually onto a cotton net base to create art nouveau patterns. Twenty-five dresses were made and displayed on mannequins at the Grant Frozen Novelties factory in a room that had once served as a storage area for broken churns. All of this is diligently recorded in company records and patent applications, as Izzy was too energetic to keep a diary.

To launch her product, the inventress held a large and decadent party in the massive freezer section of her father's factory. She called it Eskimo Night, serving bootleg liquor and leasing seals from the zoo. The animals frolicked on faux icebergs made of coconut sorbet, which floated in pools of champagne. Guests canoodled in miniature igloos.

In attendance was Amy Smith, an aspiring novelist. It is from the notes for her never-published roman à clef, *A Castle High*, that we know that Izzy arrived on a dogsled in a stunning ice-beaded raspberry frock with the phases of the moon in silver around the neckline and a dangerously short handkerchief hem.

Before the night was over, each woman scrambled to commission her own ice-beaded gown from the samples on view. Isabella Grant's weekly "freezies" became the only parties that were important, and her "icies" the thing to wear. The men donned traditional Inuit garb—elaborately embroidered sealskin parkas trimmed in fur, along with matching boots, nicknamed "Squomos."

The best part for Izzy was that the dresses melted on the way home, the ultimate in planned obsolescence. Women were forced to buy new gowns each week. Izzy furiously

ABOVE: The first-ever ice beaded dress: trimmed with depictions of the phases of the moon. Originally worn by designer Izzy Grant. Contemporary artist's interpretation.

designed fresh models, basing them on current events, just as her father did his frozen creations. But she was less literal. A pearlescent white dress with subtle navy blue pinstripes honored New York Yankee Babe Ruth's sixtieth home run. A cocoa-colored gown with a pattern of yellow ovals encircling the hips paid tribute to the low-slung skirt made of bananas that dancer Josephine Baker famously wore onstage at the Folies Bergère in Paris.

Izzy's business acumen was making her rich. Increasing numbers of moneyed youth begged to attend the freezies, and her drive for increased profits would not allow her to turn them away. As the events grew larger, the room had to be made colder to compensate for all the additional body heat. The sound of the usual party chatter was replaced by the chattering of teeth. Pale blue lips were hidden with oxblood lipstick as temperatures dipped.

The ever-increasing chill led to the denouement of the freezies, described by Smith in chapter fifty-three of *A Castle High*: "One night, the overtaxed refrigeration system failed. Minutes later, the dresses melted away. I and all the other girls were in our knickers! Since everyone was in the same boat, we just kept dancing and smoking. Who cared!? The boys sure loved it. The next week, Betty Hamilton announced an 'underwear only' party at her father's furniture factory. Since we had learned we could have just as much fun without clothes, we abandoned Izzy's freezies."

The girl who had grown rich by capitalizing on whatever was "new" had finally been felled by novelty. But Izzy Grant bounced back. In 1928, she began to build a business empire installing and repairing air conditioning units for movie theaters, hospitals, and other commercial clients. Eventually, she served as president of the Cincinnati Chamber of Commerce and became one of the city's richest women.

BELOW: Ice beaded dress inspired by popular American dancer and singer Josephine Baker's banana skirt. Contemporary artist's interpretation.

BERLIN BLACK

Daywear for the demimonde

For some denizens of the erotically charged atmosphere of Berlin's Weimar Republic cabarets, the nights were not long enough to satisfy their sexual appetites. When the clubs closed their doors at dawn, these round-the-clock sensualists donned the *Schwarzenclothen*, or "black clothing," (the word is a German-English hybrid, origin unknown) which was intended to extend the darkness, and all that was cloaked by it, into the day. The garments were not distinguished by their cut, which was standard for the time, but their hue—deeper than obsidian, darker than midnight—and their elaborate passementerie: braids, cords, beads, and fringe in the same shade as the cloth. These adornments could only be distinguished by touch, not sight, thus inviting physical contact from other *Schwarz*-wearers in the know.

And sometimes, complete strangers.

One minor American diarist, Thomas Henry, describes his first sighting of *Schwarzes*: "I was sitting at a café table and a shadow passed over me. I thought it was an eclipse of the sun, or the apocalypse. But then I saw that it was a group of twelve or so cabaret actors, in clothing so black I first thought they had been cleaning chimneys. They took up several tables nearby. They all sat very close together, and I soon noticed they were touching each other, a pretty girl with a jet-colored pageboy pressed into the lap of a lad whose outstretched arm fearlessly encircled another girl's waist. She, in turn pressed her cheek into the shoulder of a woman whose palm stroked a man's back.

"And so it went on, a human chain of touch. They made quite a spectacle. I looked for their leader, but they seemed to be an anarchic harem...no one is sultan or sultana...all are slaves to each other."

BELOW: Passementerie detail. Sensual swirls and faceted jet beads gave each garment an inviting tactility. Bloch client file. Anonymous. Ink. 1928.

BELOW: Berlin Black dress. Drawn by Bloch's assistant. Each client had a file containing several such renderings for reference when repairs or re-orders were needed. Here, embellishments are represented in white, actual dress would have been solid black. Ink. 1928.

The *Schwarzenclothen* were sewn by a blind seamstress living above a cabaret on Alexanderplatz. Her name was Elsa Bloch and she had learned her art as a young girl visiting Paris with her parents, and running her fingers over the hats in Coco Chanel's millinery shop, where her mother would discreetly deposit her every afternoon before going to meet her lover for an hour-long tryst at the Ritz Hotel.

"She thought it was a safe place to leave me while she had her assignation with an associate of my father's, so you could say Chanel was my nursemaid," Bloch said in a 1977 interview in *Paris Match,* a year before her death. "As my mother was satisfying her sensual desires, I was learning that in fashion, the feel of something is what truly distinguishes it."

Theater performers and other pillars of demimonde society were the main wearers of *Schwarzenclothen,* but it was also the choice of some workaday vamps: clerks and shopgirls who could not bear the boredom of the sunlit hours.

Bloch came to be the hands of the *Schwarzes* after sewing costumes at a small cabaret theater. In the *Paris Match* article, she describes a fitting: "A young man or woman, or sometimes a group of them, would come to my small apartment, which I understand was quite bright. I ran my hands over the body first, noticing spots where they trembled most at my touch. I then constructed a garment that lead another's hands directly to these places through a highway of cords, braids beads, and sometimes, feathers. I had an assistant who wrote the measurements."

Thomas Henry became fascinated with the polyamorous *Schwarzes* and often followed them about, recording their activities. Sometimes, they went to the cinema in an attempt to blot out the daylight. But they had to run errands like everyone else and were welcome at certain bakeries, butcher shops, and bars in borderline neighborhoods, marked discreetly with black cloth squares to indicate they were friendly to such clientele. As long as these bohemian patrons were paying, the proprietors did not seem to mind that they performed acts of frottage in front of cases displaying jelly-filled donuts.

"Sometimes I am not sure if the snowy flecks on the black clothing are a sprinkling of cocaine or a dusting of powdered sugar," Henry wrote about his subjects, who had a penchant for both sweets and mind-altering drugs, including morphine. Only once did he get the courage to reach out and touch the waist of the girl with the jet-black pageboy. "I traced my hand down what I realized was a bit of slender piping that was invisible to the naked eye, and she trembled as my fingertips neared her hipbone. Then the trolley lurched and we were separated. It is almost more tempting, more sensual, more thrilling to have this sort of encounter during the day," he wrote.

No one knew exactly how the dense Berlin Black color of the fabric and trim was created, and it was a secret Bloch took to her grave, refusing even to discuss it with *Paris Match*. Some wrongly theorized the actors simply shaved and painted their bodies, then applied the decorative touches with glue. Others said the cloth was dyed in a stew of boot black, cinders, and India ink.

Henry never discovered the formula. The rise of the Nazi party caused him to flee Berlin and spelled an end for the *Schwarzes* as well as the underground, morally amorphous world in which they lived. "Sometimes," he wrote years later. "I shut my eyes and long to see them again. They seemed a void through which one could escape into another, freer, world."

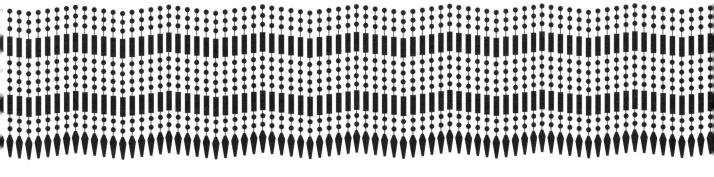

SAFARI PAJAMAS

Every night a honeymoon, every day an adventure

This khaki-colored rayon satin sleepwear for men and women was modeled after the pajamas in a 1935 Hollywood screwball comedy called *Elephant Trouble!* In the film, a spoiled American heiress honeymoons with a rugged big game hunter in Africa—but the couple's repeated attempts to consummate their union are thwarted by the antics of the hunter's pet elephant, Jinx. The actors spent most of their onscreen time in bedtime ensembles that resembled daytime safari suits complete with epaulets, expandable breast pockets, notched lapel collars, and belts. This attire satisfied Hollywood's new censorship codes and also provided fodder for humor, as Jinx often mistook the epaulet buttons for peanuts, swinging her trunk into the matrimonial bed at inopportune times.

To promote the film, the studio sold the Safari Pajamas in theater lobbies. The displays featured a life-size cardboard cutout of Jinx, her ears flaring. The first shipment sold out within a day, and it was soon apparent *Elephant Trouble!* was a hit beyond what any of the Tinsel Town moguls had imagined. When *Ladies' Home Journal* put the pajama-clad lead actress—an unknown, Jean Harlow look-alike named Ruby Demming—on the cover, the magazine had its best-selling issue in months. Demming was quoted as saying she was amazed at leading man Dex Field's expert handling of animals. Dex, interviewed on his ranchette in the San Fernando Valley, complemented Ruby's fearlessness around lions. Although, in truth, neither had gone anywhere near animals during filming.

But Middle America didn't know that. They wanted to be Ruby Demming and Dex Field. Wearing the pajamas was the closest they could get. *Elephant Trouble!* theme parties became the rage. Safari Pajamas, which were modest enough for social occasions, were de rigueur attire. Couples gathered in backyards to drink "Giraffe Juice"—rum punch served in tall highball glasses, and snack on "Jinx Mix," an assembly of various roasted nuts with a high concentration of peanuts. Women ordered multiple sets of the Safari Pajamas—for themselves and their spouses—from advertisements in *Photoplay* magazine, and the manufacturer had to add extra shifts to meet production demands. Accessories were hot sellers, too: Local sporting goods stores experienced shortages of pith helmets, binoculars, and even antivenom kits for African cobra bites.

Some women ran errands in their Safari Pajamas, citing their comfort. On weekends, men lounged in them. The reason for the public's enthusiasm was captured in a first-person column called "Babbling Babs," written by housewife Babs Donovan, and syndicated to major newspapers around the country. "Wearing them makes us feel like every night is a honeymoon night, and every day an adventure. Besides, the khaki shade flatters all complexions."

But the Serengeti sleepwear trend came to an end one day shortly before Christmas. To announce that shooting would soon begin on *More Elephant Trouble!*, the film's producers staged a publicity stunt. Fans were invited to meet Ruby, Dex, and Jinx in person at the Orpheum Theatre, a movie palace in downtown Los Angeles. Hundreds of people, many in their Safari Pajamas, showed up and spilled into the streets. "It was a seething sea of khaki satin," reads a report from the *Los Angeles Times*. "Thousands of would-be Hemingways thronging to see the stars of the hilarious hit comedy."

A radio reporter was interviewing Dex and Ruby live on air when Jinx suddenly broke free and knocked over the Safari Pajama display. She trampled her cardboard doppelganger—the sight of which animal experts later said might have incited her rampage—sending people and pajamas scattering in all directions. An excerpt from the radio show transcript:

OPPOSITE: Costume design sketch for actor Dex Field's attire in *Elephant Trouble!* Jinx the elephant also pictured. Anonymous movie studio staff artist. Watercolor. 1934.

BELOW: Costume design sketch for actress Ruby Demming's attire in *Elephant Trouble!* Note the pink fuzzy slippers and matching canteen cover. Anonymous movie studio staff artist. Watercolor. 1934.

Ruby: Stop her, Dex! She's heading into the crowd.

Reporter: Oh the humanity!

Dex: She's not really my goddamn elephant. You were on set. Do you think what you see on that screen is real? [unintelligible] Are you an idiot? I'm as much an elephant wrangler as you are a blushing wedding night virgin.

Ruby: You arrogant coward. [Sound of impact, possibly Ruby's handbag against Dex's head.]

Reporter: Ladies and gentlemen! Watch it! Get out of the way!

Dex: She's coming this way. Run!

Reporter: The people. They're running. They're screaming. Oh ladies and gentlemen…I have to step away for a minute. Oh, this is the worst thing I've ever witnessed.

Amazingly enough, no one was harmed in the rampage, especially considering that Jinx was recaptured several blocks from the Orpheum, in the rotunda of Los Angeles City Hall. The only serious injuries were to the reputation of Dex Field and the sales figures for the Safari Pajamas. After Dex's distinctly unheroic words were broadcast, the *Elephant Trouble!* films were cancelled, and Safari Pajamas sales slumped. The sudden surplus of satin sleepwear was donated to a charity that shipped it to an actual African country, where it was shredded and turned into mosquito netting to protect against malaria.

FIDELITY CARDIGAN

Button up for victory!

1943

The first Fidelity Cardigan was created by Caroline Hart, the founding member of a Shaker, Ohio, knitting circle that made socks for American military men serving overseas in World War II. After hearing stories from the other girls about the difficulties of remaining faithful to their soldier sweethearts, Hart, who did not have a beau—Army, Navy, Air Force, or otherwise—pledged to design a pattern for a knitted garment that would help her friends stay true.

The sweaters were drab in color; made of thick, rough yarn; and poorly fitted: design elements thought to repel men. They stood in stark contrast to the tight, waist-skimming knitwear that had been brought into vogue by the era's yarn shortages. Young women were hesitant to wear them at first, but the energetic Hart encouraged it in the name of patriotism and asked a local "Buy War Bonds" campaign to display the knitting patterns beside their promotional materials at banks and grocery stores. "The Fidelity Cardigan is all about my love of country," Hart said in a newspaper interview with the *Shaker Times.* The accompanying photograph shows a plain but tidy girl wearing a boxy, gray sweater and holding a small American flag.

Press agents in the War Department saw the article and got Hart's permission distribute her knitting patterns nationwide. They printed thousands of brochures with instructions for making the cardigan, even adding the slogan, "Button Up for Victory!" The "Sweetheart Sweater," as it was sometimes called, became quite popular in knitting circles across the U.S. This lead to rituals Hart had not anticipated. In one, a girl who strayed plucked a single button from the cardigan and sent it to her man. Soldiers

BELOW: Flat of the Fidelity Cardigan. Thought to be by Caroline Hart. Pencil. 1943.

Preliminary sketch of the Fidelity Cardigan for a War Department "Buy Bonds" brochure. Anonymous WPA artist. Watercolor. 1943.

nicknamed them "heartbreak bullets" and loaded them into their weapons; an enemy kill a way to avenge a girl's honor.

Naysayers living stateside claimed the cardigans were not patriotic at all. A letter to the editor of the *Shaker Times* read: "In a time of rationing, why should one of the things never in short supply—the beauty of young women—be as dear as butter?" Others had similar complaints.

But the Fidelity Cardigan, thanks to its strong association with patriotism, continued to grow in popularity. In an effort to bump up bond sales even further, the War Department held a contest for Miss Fidelity USA; the winner was to make personal appearances across the country, selling bonds and sitting in on knitting circles. The contest proved disastrous for the fidelity aspect of the cardigans. Girls wanted to look their best for the competition, and so discarded Hart's original instructions. Instead they chose candy hues and soft fibers. Some skilled knitters even added darts to show off their bustlines or belts to highlight slim waists.

The next newspaper articles show the Miss Fidelity USA finalists, a row of pretty young women beaming at the camera, some of whom appear to be in cashmere. Hart is just visible in the background, sitting with the panel of judges, and looking slightly shell-shocked. The winning entry was a cardigan of fine-gauge, blush pink angora, its plunging neckline and slim fit empasizing the hourglass shape of its creator, Betty Anderson.

On her tour of the U.S,. accompanied by Caroline Hart, Betty was photographed frequently and became something of a pinup girl—much to the dismay of her fiancé, private first class Donald Smith, who was serving somewhere in Europe. On the second week of the tour, it was leaked to the press that in every town she visited, Betty was engaging in movie theater mash sessions with the first 4-F man to look in her direction. The scandalous gossip proved the undoing of the Sweetheart Sweater. Patriotic American girls suddenly feared that wearing them would ruin their reputations. In the months after the scandal broke, American GIs received socks knit from the most luxurious of yarns, in colors like cotton candy pink, lemon drop yellow, and pistachio taffy green.

FORGOTTEN FASHION

HAVANA OYSTER DIGGER

A post-war antidote to olive drab

These men's shorts were the cornerstone of Operation Paradise, a clandestine post–World War II effort by the U.S. government to help ease returning soldiers back into civilian life. Marketed by the Pentagon under the brand name Beach Pals, each style was designed to promote relaxation with a name that evoked a vacation haven bordered by sand and sea. But there was more to their lulling effect than a simple holiday-esque moniker.

Although the patterns in the fabric appeared to be the fanciful abstract shapes that were to become so popular in the 1950s, they were actually based on the ten Rorschach inkblots, tweaked somewhat to subconsciously evoke the most universally positive responses. "When veterans look down at their shorts and find themselves musing on pleasant things like women, steak, and eight-cylinder engines, it will help calm their minds and restore their love of country," wrote General Frank Erickson in a recently declassified letter to Millicent Jones, a junior designer at Sears, Roebuck & Co. who was recruited by the Pentagon to create the line.

Swatches from Operation Paradise files show that Jones gave the minimally colored Rorschach inkblot patterns a more up-to-date, tropical flair. The Waikiki Wader had an aloha sunset palette of pinks and blues, swirling into shapes that created the suggestion of a surf and turf platter. The Monaco High-Tider's refined color scheme of oyster pearl white and tuxedo black, with a shot of salmon pink, coalesced into what to the knowing eye is a tumult of reclining women. The Havana Oyster Digger was a riot of red and other sizzling Cuban shades in which swam an inkblot-like version of the 1948 Cadillac, propelled by its tailfin. The Miami Catamaraner was a wave of hot oranges and splashy turquoises that combined

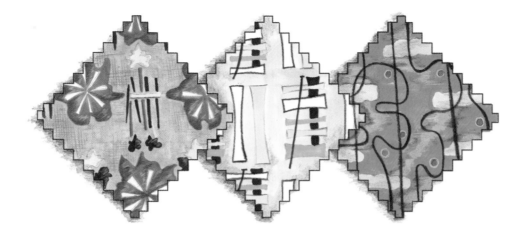

all three of General Erickson's requirements into an orgy of abstract happiness.

Other design elements of the shorts echoed the trouble-free feel of the disguised Rorschach patterns: easy care cotton-nylon blend fabric, a simple zipper/button fastener combination, and numerous pockets.

Beach Pals were sold in shopping centers near subdivisions developed for those buying houses on the GI Bill. They flew off shelves, reflecting men's hunger for anything bright, loud, and garish after years in olive drab. This desire is echoed in the simultaneous explosion in popularity of two other men's fashion items: the brightly colored Hawaiian shirt, which was typically covered with more representational images such as plumeria flowers, flames, marine fauna, and island women; and the wide, hand-painted tie, which depicted fantasy scenes such as beautiful Tahitian girls playing poker under palm trees.

Often, men paired one or both of these with Beach Pals shorts. This was the aesthetic equivalent of dropping the atomic bomb, but the U.S. government didn't care. Reports sent to General Erickson from Operation Paradise field representatives were positive. In the neighborhoods where the shorts were sold, the lawns grew thicker and greener, the PTA meetings more crowded, the bake sales bountiful. Jones moved into a small office in the Pentagon and was hard at work making the next series of shorts, which included the Cape Cod Crop, an autumn model perfect for raking leaves, with a colorway of rust and brown, and a pattern that contained subliminal images of a pretty girl eating tri-tip.

But another branch of the federal government, the U.S. Commerce Department, was not happy with Operation Paradise. Economists pointed out that a deep sense of contentment could go too far. Minirecessions were taking place in the communities saturated with the wave of Waikiki Waders and other models. The men were too satisfied. They lacked motivation. They were happy enough watering lawns and teaching their children how to ride tricycles, but these pleasures were shutting down the assembly lines of America's proudest resource, ambition.

This over-strong sense of well-being was deemed a threat to national security, and Operation Paradise was shut down. Millicent Jones was employed by a burgeoning surf-wear manufacturer to adapt the Bermuda short to the U.S. market. General Erickson, deemed by higher-ups to understand a bit about Cuba from his experience with the Beach Pals, was put in charge of creating an attack scenario for the small island nation, although no one thought it would ever be needed.

BELOW: A recently declassified U.S. government technical illustration of the Havana Oyster Digger.

OPPOSITE. Fabric patterns showing various interpretations of the Rorschach inkblots. Colored pencil. 1947.

FRIGIDAIRE FORMALS

Sometimes, it all begins with a muse.

When Gaston Darchez first laid eyes on Kaitlyn Anderson, she was removing a silver tray of Jell-O parfaits from a sparkling new 1950 Frigidaire Imperial refrigerator. Kaitlyn was six feet tall, with flame-red hair and skin so white that it had been alternately described by her series of minor poet boyfriends as "milky," "snowy," "ghostly," or by the less metaphorically inclined, "pale." Her long spine gave her a slightly concave posture, which had once led her pediatrician to predict a lifetime of expensive medical treatments. But by the time twenty-one-year-old Kaitlyn crossed Darchez's line of vision, her backbone had become her fortune.

Kaitlyn was one of the few people in the world with the innate ability to hold her torso in a nearly perpetual C-curve, which at the time was considered the ultimate posture of a high-fashion model. She had been discovered by an art director and embarked on a very successful career posing for illustrated magazine advertisements. It was in this capacity that Darchez, an expatriate French former fashion designer, first saw her. He had been hired to draw the ad for the 1950 Frigidaire Imperial. Kaitlyn had been contracted to be part of the picture. Her elegant form, swathed in a sky blue ball gown and curved over the tray of gelatin treats, suggested that the icy confines of the refrigerator emitted breezes that could transform anyone's life into a glamorous one and give pedigree to even the most pedestrian desserts.

For Darchez, the scene was simply a series of colors and shapes to be put on paper, until the moment Kaitlyn unwound from her C-curve and stood up straight. "She dominated the entire room," he wrote. "And I knew what I had to do to become a fashion designer again: go big." The Frenchman had worked in all the great Parisian fashion ateliers, but was never chosen as an assistant, and so had come to the United States, bitter and angry, promising to abandon couture and "become an illustrator of the hulking monstrous machines and the lazy and wasteful women who use them." But in truth he was haunted by the popularity of Christian Dior's New Look of 1947 and longed to create a style that would have the same meteoric impact on fashion.

At the sight of Kaitlyn beside the modern icebox, he decided "hope lies in hugeness." The drawing studio had the same high ceilings as the abodes of the Parisian elite—Darchez's desired customers. He knew that all of these privileged women harbored the same secret wish: to enter the elaborate parties held in these cavernous rooms in gowns so stunning they would make all the other guests blend into the parquet floors. To become their next design darling, Darchez would have to make dresses that would dominate these spaces like no one before him: evening gowns on a gargantuan scale. "Double doors will become triples to accommodate their entrances, and grand staircases will look like matchstick ladders beside them," he wrote. "I will transform every woman into Kaitlyn."

He convinced her to sign a contract to pose for sketches in the studio after hours. During their sessions, he gave her playful nicknames: "The Glacier," "The Iceberg," "Mon Petit Mont Blanc," all of which he wrote in a brushy stroke beside his drawings of her. It is from Darchez's sketchbook that we know much about the development of the dresses, which the designer called Frigidaire Formals.

Like Kaitlyn and the appliances, the collection was white in color and grand in scale. The foundation of each gown was a fitted bodice that emphasized a woman's hourglass silhouette. This was enhanced by design features that extended the garment's volume in all directions: a ball-gown skirt with a twenty-foot circumference, translucent chiffon "poet" sleeves with nearly as much yardage as a

BELOW: "La Glacière" (The Icebox). The large scale of the gown was typical of the Frigidaire Formals collection. Gaston Darchez. Gouache. 1950.

parachute, stand-up raw silk collars that reached above the ears, satin trains so long they practically required a caboose. In the drawings, Kaitlyn stands not in her popular C-curve, but regally upright, a pose surely requested by Darchez to enhance the large scale of the gowns. She is particularly fetching in earlier designs such as "La Glacière" (The Icebox), a dress and cape combination that reveals the impact of appliances on Darchez's work. The floor-length porcine cape clasps at the neck with a silver lever modeled after a Frigidaire door handle. Beneath it is a ball gown, the warm ivory moiré silk glowing like the light from inside a refrigerator. Kaitlyn smiles slyly at the artist, one hand touched to the cape's upturned collar.

But the gigantic scale of the dresses relied on more than generous swaths of fabric modeled by a statuesque goddess. For all the drawing and fitting sessions, "The Iceberg" wore five-inch pumps. Sketches show that Darchez began with three-inch heels and modified them to increase the height. He gave much thought to the engineering, reinforcing the shoes with a steel shank so they would not snap and send his muse tumbling. One might assume that this footwear was the cause of the pinched look that began to appear on Kaitlyn's face one-third of the way through the sketchbook. But one would be wrong.

After many weeks of the boardlike posture, Kaitlyn was having difficulty forming her trademark C-curve when she posed for the appliance illustrations, which were her main source of income. Art directors complained. One can find fewer representations of her russet-haired presence in magazine advertisements from this period, and it can be assumed Kaitlyn was probably suffering financially as a result. But she was trapped in her contract with Darchez, and in his dresses, which just got bigger and bigger. In the sketch for "Le Gaz," which drew its name and shape from the white-hot flame flickering from gas stove burners, her face is nearly lost amid a flurry of ostrich feathers built up around her as if she is the center of a blaze. Even in Darchez's stylized hand, one notices her visage sports a scowl, and her pale skin is slightly pink.

The final straw was "La Lave," a dress-within-a-dress clearly inspired by the era's top-loading dishwashers, in which cups and plates were placed in a cylindrical wire basket and submerged in a tube beneath the kitchen counter. The innermost gown was a tightly fitted sheath, made of fabric Darchez designed, white silk embroidered in silver thread that formed an abstract pattern suggesting the wire cage. Over this was a layer of suds-inspired translucent chiffon. This was topped by a porcelain white evening coat in a tubular shape, which appeared to transform Kaitlyn into a Doric column. Around the figure of Kaitlyn, Darchez has limned the Parthenon, complete with the row of massive white columns lining its façade. Kaitlyn, in the dress, becomes one of them. Her face atop it is like that of an angry goddess.

It is the last dress in the portfolio of the Frigidaire Formal collection. Tucked behind it is half of a torn contract—the one Darchez had with Kaitlyn. It is obvious the designer could not go on without his muse. If his dresses were ever actually produced, there is no record of them. His Frigidaire Formals drifted into oblivion, as did he.

But it was not his mammoth and towering creations that could have made his fortune, it was what lay beneath them: his carefully engineered footwear. In 1952, the term "stiletto" was coined to describe the high-heeled shoe with the spiky heel bolstered by a metal shank. Its popularity was attributed mainly to Roger Vivier, who worked for the designer Darchez had so envied: Christian Dior.

OPPOSTIE: "Le Gaz," (The Gas Flame). Portfolio drawing by Gaston Darchez for his Frigidaire Formals collection. Gouache. 1950.

BELOW: "La Lave" (The Washing Machine). Note that model Kaitlyn Anderson is equated with a column in the Parthenon. Gaston Darchez. Gouache. 1950.

POLY-CHEM OXFORD

Martinis, mad scientists, and the problem with perfection

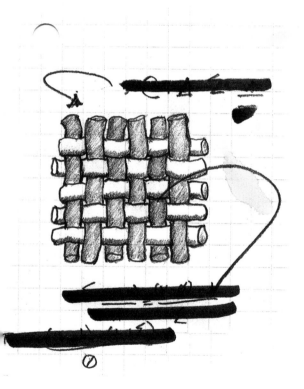

ABOVE: Detail view of fabric weave for Poly-Chem Oxford. Anonymous. Mechanical pencil on graph paper. 1953.

OPPOSITE: Sketch of Poly-Chem Oxford and partial rendering of the mysterious chemical formula invented to make the fabric. Attributed to Chet Thompson. Mechanical pencil on graph paper. 1953.

The goal of the Poly-Chem Oxford Project, undertaken by a team of MIT-educated chemists at Tri-Lab, a now-shuttered private research facility in Cambridge, Massachusetts was to produce "a fifty-year businessman's shirt" so indestructible that it would last half a century. When the beta fabric was first created in the lab, it was such perfection that the team was initially afraid they had reproduced "the skin of God." From team leader Chet Thompson's diary: "We sat around after that: Bob, Mike, Dave, and me, in the bar of a steak place called The Carriage House, drinking martinis and wondering if we'd changed the world—if His wrath would rain down on us. Then Bob said maybe the first guys who invented alcohol felt the same way, and we all lightened up."

The fabric was shipped to a garment factory where a hundred samples of the shirts were constructed, based on a popular classic Brooks Brothers cut. When they arrived back at Tri-Lab and were subjected to laboratory tests, the shirts seemed magical: They repelled stains, the buttons never popped off, and the fabric was so durable that pocket protectors were unnecessary. They even seemed to stop perspiration. No longer would it be crucial to keep a stack of freshly laundered and folded shirts in an office drawer in order to have something to wear after spending a night at work.

Chet Thompson wrote in his lab notes, "With this shirt, we may have achieved the sartorial version of immortality."

It seemed like everyone at Tri-Lab was going to get very, very rich. The team began referring to themselves as "The New Brooks Brothers." But Thompson knew the Poly-Chem Oxford had to be field-tested for durability. For help, he phoned MIT PhD chemistry candidate Burton Trallway, who had become a sort of team mascot, hanging around the lab, doing chores, and offering suggestions. Trallway lived in a large, dilapidated Victorian house and was known for his wild parties that mixed fraternity brothers with studious types, faculty with freshman, and elderly neighbors with artists.

Before the party, each male guest was given a shirt, and its miraculous technologically advanced properties were explained to him.

When his guests had left, Trallway recorded his impressions into a large reel-to-reel tape recorder he kept in his living room. From the transcript: "I do not know if I have held the most successful or dullest party in the history of Cambridge, Massachusetts. No one spilled or broke anything. Not one cigarette burn in my upholstery. And I heard very few if any impassioned debates."

At The Carriage House the next morning, the Poly-Chem Oxford team met as they usually did post-bash, but as they ordered a round of Bloody Marys they realized that they had no hangovers. No one had overindulged the night before. Trallway described his findings and the team had to agree:

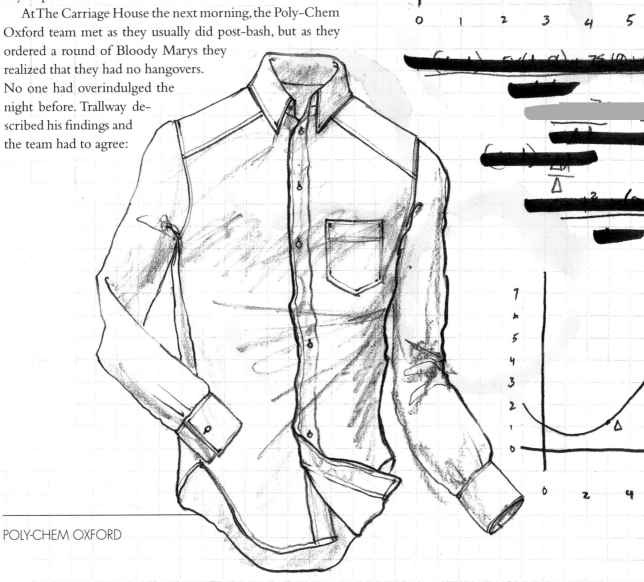

POLY-CHEM OXFORD

There had been something odd about the party. But did it have anything to do with the shirts?

Hoping the event had been an anomaly, they had more Poly-Chem Oxfords made, and distributed the indestructible shirts at several other get-togethers. But the result was always the same. Docility overcame the guests. Caution entered conversation. People retired early, always going home with the same person with whom they had arrived.

The team tried other field settings: giving Poly-Chem Oxfords to college students and office workers. In some cases, the recipients returned the shirts claiming they itched or were cut too tight. But Thompson knew this was not the case.

"Much as I despise the so-called 'science' of psychology, our field tests conclude that when people know they are in the presence of perfection—indeed, when this very perfection shrouds their bodies—they are more conscious of their mistakes, sloppiness, and trespasses. The constant reminder of the gap between the perfection of the shirt and the flaws of the wearer make it impossible to take pleasure in life while wearing the shirt. Plus there is the added stress that the shirt might outlive you."

The team concluded that the Poly-Chem Oxford could not be brought to market. Every copy of the formula for the chemical that made up the fabric was shredded. It was a huge disappointment, and they spent many evenings for the next two months at The Carriage House.

"We did make the skin of God," Thompson wrote, years later. "And no one felt worthy of wearing it." Some vintage clothes dealers say that occasionally, a perfectly crisp Oxford-style shirt turns up at a Cambridge-area Goodwill, with no tag inside the collar: one of the original Poly-Chems, still as fresh as the day it was first worn.

FOUR O'CLOCK DRESS

For abject and idle afternoons

Not a day dress, and not an evening gown, this toga-like garment was worn by mid-century American housewives during the single, lonely, long-shadowed hour after the pot roast was placed in the oven but before a husband's key was heard in the front door. Made of light-reflecting fabrics such as satin or sharkskin in bright period colors like Miami-limeade, Flamingo-pink, or Navajo-turquoise, it was meant to provoke optimism in the wearer.

ABOVE: Combination shoulder clasp/makeup compact, open to show rouge in rare "Russian Red" shade. Brevi studio. Gouache. 1957.

BELOW: The secret pocket that proved the undoing of the "Foursie" dress. Brevi studio. Gouache. 1957.

The dress was held in place at the shoulder with a clasp that doubled as a makeup compact. This opened to reveal a more risqué shade of rouge than would be worn at other times of day. Each "Foursie" also had secret inner pockets to hide the tools of whatever vice occupied the otherwise abject and idle afternoon. Contents often included miniature gin bottles, marijuana joints, or palm-sized erotic novels.

Worn only in affluent suburbs reached by the commuter trains of New York City, the Four O'clock Dress was the concept of Jacques Brevi, a French couturier who trained in the Paris atelier of Hubert de Givenchy but came to the United States in the mid-1950s. Soon disillusioned with the grime of the bongo-playing milieu of the Lower East Side, he decamped to the affluent suburb of Bronxville, which, he wrote to a friend, was "paradise with Cadillacs" but one that he feared was not safe from the "dirty fingers of nihilism."

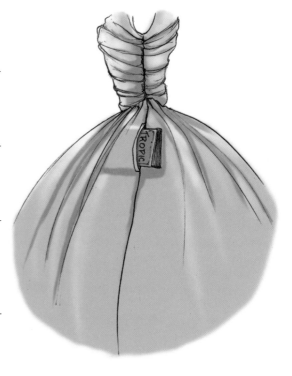

Brevi set to work preserving his suburban haven by creating a dress that would, "if not give meaning to life, then distract from the fact that there is none." He imported the brilliantly colored material from the finest Italian mills, hired students from Sarah Lawrence College as seamstresses, and sold his creations in at least seven shops in Westchester County. The distinct rustling sound of the brilliant togas became

BELOW: Toga-influenced Four O'clock Dress, in "Navajo-turquoise" colored silk. Jacques Brevi, private portfolio. Gouache. 1957.

known in better neighborhoods as "the laughter of the dresses," as Technicolor Athenas emerged from their houses and congregated on cherry-blossom drenched front lawns to trade hits of Indonesian reefer, sip crème de menthe, and read aloud from annotated bootleg copies of *Tropic of Cancer*.

Soon, the women began to expand the secret sartorial compartments to include heavier items such as law books and manifestos. Brevi warned that the garments were not designed for this and would not be able to withstand it. In April of 1957, his prediction came true when New Haven resident Carol Jones weighed down her chartreuse "Foursie" with copies of *Atlas Shrugged* and a three-hundred-page letter to the editor of the *Westchester County Times* espousing individual freedom. The inner pocket ripped, and the contents fell and crushed several of her toes, leaving her prone and unconscious from pain in her foyer.

The next day, the incident was reported in the very paper in which Carol had wished to publish her letter. Her husband, Charles Jones, was quoted as saying: "A man should not come home to the smell of burning dinner and the shocking sight of an incapacitated wife. I blame these glorified bed sheets." Clippings of the story were found on the pillows of most Westchester housewives. The Four O'clock Dress was soon known as the "divorce dress" and sales plummeted. Brevi wrote to a friend, "I suppose I will once again pull up my silver tent stakes and take the circus of my life elsewhere." He moved to Vermont, where he made sandals.

Note: In areas closer to Manhattan, the garment was known as the "Three-thirty Dress," as the commuter trains arrived earlier.

CASSIDY TROUSER SUIT

Designed for girl subway buskers

Most people have never heard of the Trouser Wars of 1964, probably because they didn't actually happen. The fictional sartorial skirmishes were the invention of a Madison Avenue advertising executive named Donald Fielding. He was inspired by the very real fashion battle between the Mods and Rockers in Great Britain that same year—in which Vespa-riding dandies faced off against motorcycle-straddling devotees of the leather jacket, creating panic among ordinary citizens. Fielding's "wars" took place in Greenwich Village and were part of an elaborate marketing campaign to promote the Cassidy, a woman's trouser suit that was in desperate need of distinguishing itself in a fall fashion season suddenly awash in an unexpected sea of trouser suits.

The Cassidy was the signature piece of an original line created at a high-end Greenwich Village boutique called Bird, Bread, & Soul, which carried clothing inspired by the American folk music revival. Available in houndstooth wool check, in shades of coffee or Chianti, the Cassidy paired a narrow pant with a fitted jacket with set-in sleeves. Ostensibly designed for girl subway buskers, the price point made it more likely to be worn by those whose guitar cases overflowed with inherited wealth rather than appreciatively tossed coinage. Suede patches on the torso protected against the wear and tear of "constant contact" with a guitar. Velvet-covered buttons prevented scratches on one's banjo. Underarm vents and elbow grommets allowed air circulation and increased motility during the vigorous strumming required for rousing choruses of songs such as "If I Had a Hammer."

It was worn with "Busker Boots," ankle boots with washed leather uppers and rubber soles to promote comfort during long periods spent standing on cement subway platforms.

Each Cassidy came with a coordinating guitar strap and a bracelet that was actually a miniature tambourine.

Although very on-trend, the Cassidy was not selling well. The owner and designer of all the merchandise at Bird, Bread, & Soul, Carol Day, had only a small budget for advertising. Her fortunes changed when she had a chance encounter with Donald Fielding at a gallery opening, and he agreed to take on her campaign pro bono.

His reasons are made clear in a transcription from a Dictaphone recording, one of hundreds Fielding made daily throughout the 1960s. "I can now test the advertising theory I have always believed to be true. To love a product, people need to know it has an enemy, a sinister force, working against it. By buying it, they will feel they are on the side of good. Marlboro could have tripled their sales by introducing a rustler to steal the cowboy's horses. Snap, Crackle, and Pop needed a Silence, Muffle, and Quiet to challenge them, *West Side Story* style, in gang warfare over the territory of the cereal bowl."

What better enemy for the all-American, folk music-loving Cassidy, Fielding reasoned, than a trouser suit emblematic of the other surging force in popular music, the British Invasion? Fielding dubbed the nonexistent garment the Royal Trouser Suit, and its imaginary wearer a decadent, shallow, arrogant English party girl who resented the Cassidy's folksy American honesty so much that she harassed her in the streets.

Knowing the public was primed for such a tale thanks to the media obsession with the Mod/Rocker conflict, he planned to spread the fable of the Trouser Wars through a whisper campaign. He asked Day to draw up a sketch of the Royal Trouser Suit so he would have a mental picture of it—a personal visual reference that would help keep his fantastic stories consistent. She limned a sister suit to the Cassidy, but made of velvet tartan. Sheared mink patches on the torso protected it from the wear and tear of constant contact

ABOVE: The Cassidy Trouser Suit with model depicted in a rare non-confrontational composition. Carol Day. Colored pencil. 1964.

RIGHT: Cassidy bracelet, a mini-tambourine.

OPPOSITE: Royal Trouser Suite and Royal bracelet with spikes. Carol Day. Colored pencil. 1964.

with expensive handbags. Coats of arms emblazoned on the buttons scratched those who came too close. It came with matching gloves and a bracelet that was actually a miniature spiked dog collar.

It was worn with "Peasant Kickers," patent leather ankle boots with pointed toes.

Day's delightful sketches, tucked away for years by Fielding, show the suits in actual battle scenes from the Trouser Wars. The penultimate drawing is of a haughty young aristocratic woman tossing a cigarette butt into a Cassidy girl's open guitar case as she kicks her houndstooth-clad shin.

Every day at lunch, Fielding took the bus from his Madison Avenue office to Washington Square Park to feed the pigeons and spread rumors about the Trouser Wars. Fielding was pleased the first time he overheard someone at a coffee shop discussing the terrible Royals.

There was an op-ed in *The Village Voice* deploring the violence and arrogance of the invaders. Someone even wrote to *The New York Times* expressing hope that Lady Bird Johnson would wear the Cassidy as an example of American pride. Some street musicians penned songs about the suit, likening the wearers to the minutemen. The Cassidy flew off the racks. Carol Day expressed her gratitude to Fielding. She promised that she would rename one of her spring shirts, which had a working title of the "Tom Dooley," the "Don Fielding."

But then Fielding made a startling discovery that is best revealed to the reader in a direct transcription of his Dictaphone recording: "Today, I saw a Royal. A real Royal. I don't understand. Where did she come from? I was feeding the pigeons as usual when a girl walked by and kicked them—in Peasant Kickers! She had the velvet tartan suit, the vengeful look, the whole thing. We made them up. How can she exist?" A quick stroll around the archway in Washington Square Park revealed a group of Royals, smoking and staring maliciously at innocent Cassidys, some of whom were actually playing acoustic guitar.

Fielding decided he must put an end to things before anyone was hurt, and the only way to do it was to find who was making the Royal Trouser Suit and Peasant Kickers. Just around the corner from Bird, Bread, & Soul, he found a new boutique with a purple façade and large gold letters over the door reading "Frug & Scepter." Behind the counter, her long blonde hair hidden under a Vidal Sassoon geometric wig, was Carol Day, and on the racks were rows of tartan velvet. As described by Fielding in a Dictaphone recording, "I fled, randomly at first. Zigzagging through the streets like a madman. Then I knew what to do."

The next tape is missing. But that evening, both boutiques burned to the ground. Some saw a man in a gray flannel suit, clutching what looked like a paper bag of bird seed, fleeing the scene, but Fielding was never accused of arson. Thankfully, no one was harmed in the twin fires, and the Trouser Wars of 1964 remained as they were meant to be: imaginary, without a drop of blood spilled or a seam torn. By 1968, Day had used her insurance money to open a boutique, which she named Fringe, in San Francisco's Haight-Ashbury neighborhood. Fielding's only other notable career achievement was to work as a consultant for Richard Nixon's presidential campaign, although some say the rumors of the Royal were partial inspiration for punk fashion fifteen years later.

BEIGE LAMÉ

Swinging London meets the aristocratic mini

The Swinging Sixties sent London socialites and shopgirls alike into the glimmering embrace of the gold or silver lamé mini dress. But for one member of the gentry, Lady Amelia Betterly, the gowns inspired no affection. She thought they made her peers look "like tarts, dressed by gusts of wind in bits of discarded Christmas wrapping," and said so in a diary entry from December 1967. For her Kensington clique, eight girls who had been friends since childhood, she wanted something stylish but not vulgar. And so Lady Amelia hit on the idea of beige lamé, and had several bolts made and sewn into dresses at the family textile mill in Rajasthan.

Although not as eye-catching as the more precious metallics, beige lamé earned the "Betterly Girls" an unanticipated degree of notoriety. The sight of their thin silhouettes, ghostly pale for want of outdoor activity and encased in the nearly colorless material, made quite an impact. As described by poet and society columnist Beatrice White, a regular that winter at Chelsea house parties: "Entering the room together, the octet brought to mind an exotic, aquarium-kept, albino octopus—lank, lazy, lithe, tossing themselves of a piece onto a reef-like expanse of floor pillows and remaining there for the evening, occasionally raising a milky tentacle, staring about the room

BELOW: Eight versions of the Beige Lamé mini, worn by the octet of society girls known as the Wan Lamés. Lady Amelia, the designer, is seen center, kneeling. Anonymous. *British Vogue*. Ink and watercolor. 1968.

with their large eyes as if hoping to draw microscopic nourishment from the air but not really caring if they did or not."

They became known as the Wan Lamés, and, for two months in early 1968, were the talk of the town. The Wans rarely spoke (some less-kind observers said opinions had been bred out of them) or exerted themselves physically. In school, this had earned them the label "dull," but in a world mad for iconoclastic chatter and endless frantic hours of freeform dancing, their reticent stillness was a welcome relief and created an aura of mystery. "Who are these girls who dare be silent when change is on everyone's lips?" White said in a column.

Gaining the spotlight in such a wild age made the Wans a source of envy, and the beige lamé dresses were soon copied. But the second wave of girls, who always traveled in groups of eight, could not maintain the reserve of the original Betterly Wans, who soon left the scene, entering into marital engagements or becoming ever so slightly more active in charitable work.

The dresses soared in popularity, and the Wan Wars began as boutiques competed to offer the most pallid version of the mini. White observed: "The beige has been completely stripped away, so the dresses now appear platinum, and are so highly reflective that they are garish, the complete opposite of Lady Amelia's intent." They were so bright that a group of eight mini-clad girls crossing Kings Road sent out a glare strong enough to temporarily blind a passing motorist, causing a fatal car accident and commencing the end of the trend.

Both an anonymous donation to the dead man's family and an unsigned letter deriding the dresses (published in the *Daily Mirror* and unfortunately headlined "Dressed to Kill" by the editor) were thought to be from Lady Amelia. One of her original beige lamé minis remains on display at her parents' house in Earls Terrace, which is open Tuesdays through Fridays for prearranged tours in order to help the Betterlys pay property taxes. The Rajasthan mill can also be visited, as Lady Amelia has transformed it into an ashram for wealthy American tourists.

PONCHETTES

Stylish clothes for spiritual quests

In midwinter 1970, accompanied by the sound of a single electric guitar, a line of lissome, uncannily suntanned models strode across the carpet of the Miss Bergdorf junior salon, the teen section of Manhattan's landmark luxury department store. The impressions their bare feet left in the carpet were faint, but for a small audience of adolescent girls looking for meaning in uncertain times, the impact of their ensembles was anything but.

This was the debut fashion show of Margaret Anne Avery, a Parsons Design School dropout and trust fund orphan who had spent the previous summer searching for "a way to make clothes with meaning." She had meditated at Mayan pyramids, prayed at Tibetan Buddhist temples, backstroked in the Ganges, and finally spun with the Islamic Sufis in Morocco, who whirled much like the Turkish dervishes. After one particularly dizzying day, she was informed that the name "Sufi" was derived from the Arabic word for "wool" because of the simple garments the devotees wore to show their asceticism.

Eureka. She had a purpose for her clothing: a collection that would outfit the Western customer for a spiritual quest—in a stylish way.

The anchor piece was an ankle-length tunic with bell sleeves. Made of lightweight yet durable waxed khaki cotton, it was tough enough to climb steep mountain trails, yet the decorative embroidered placket at the neckline, and matching trim at the sleeve-ends and hem, helped make one presentable when meeting the hermetic guru at the top. It was called a "Quest-an"—a caftan worn on a quest. Other items included a "Ponchette" (a shortened boiled wool poncho for less arduous journeys), a "Pilgrimage Tunic" (a hardy quilted nylon vest that doubled as a rain shelter and sleeping bag), and

LEFT: Ponchette over waffle-weave body-stocking. Catalogue for "Sit-In for Style" fashion show at Bergdorf Goodman, Manhattan. Margaret Anne Avery. 1970.

a "Bathing Burnoose" (a hooded terry cloth robe for warming up after swimming in sacred rivers).

Avery chose a limited palette in colors she dubbed "sand," "storm," and "clarity" (beige, gray, and white) so they could easily mix and match during long sojourns "where one's only closet was a backpack and one's only thoughts were of enlightenment." All the garments could be worn with another of Avery's original creations: a waffle-weave long john that was cut much like a Union suit but made with a knit blend so it recalled the late-1960s body stocking.

Avery was able to show her clothes at Bergdorf's because her parents, before their tragic deaths in a balloon accident, had been loyal customers. The only press to attend was a reporter for a one-sheet mimeographed underground newspaper, *Freaky Folks Tidings*, which had begun as a music calendar listing but later expanded to include gossip about the local rock music scene, and was there to report on the guitarist providing the accompaniment. The paper was a collective, and all stories were bylined "Everyman."

From the article, we know that the show was dubbed "A Sit-In for Style" to capitalize on the era's popular form of social protest. No chairs were provided, just floor pillows. Sandalwood incense wafted through the air over the strains of the electric guitar. One employee taped over the middle two letters in the sign on the wall that read "Miss" so that it would instead say "Ms." It was obvious the department managers were attempting to incorporate as many elements of the counterculture as possible into the show.

The models were styled to look like Avery, who had a distinctly road-weary sex appeal: a deep tan, straight hair sparkling with sun-kissed streaks, fingers be-ringed with sterling silver, and a gaunt frame from subsisting on street vendor food, dried apricots, and the occasional Belgian chocolate. Each wore a backpack that jingled with both practical D rings and magical amulets. The clothes, and the meaningful life they promised, were such a hit they sold out within hours. Soon, privileged girls were traveling the globe in Avery's creations. This type was nicknamed, rather derisively by less-moneyed travelers, a "Ponchette." She stayed at the best *riads* in Fez, dropped chlorine tablets in the Jordan River before even dipping a toe into its storied waters, and slept "rough" at sacred sites after bodyguards had sprayed the area with insecticide and snake repellant. She hired Sherpas not just for their strong backs but for their wit and good looks. She traveled barefoot in first class on jet airplanes.

Meanwhile, Avery, the designer who had made all of this possible, established an atelier in a Greenwich Village brownstone. Amid smoky curlicues of burning sage, she planned a collection based entirely on Mexican *huipiles* tunics whose stripes and patterns revealed one's life story and purpose. But toward the end of summer, her peaceful retreat was invaded. Not finding answers on their travels, the Ponchettes returned to New York and tracked down Avery. They became more than customers. The were followers—waiting outside her apartment and shadowing her on the streets straining to hear her utter bits of wisdom. They hoped her next collection might provide answers they had not found on their travels.

Eventually unnerved by the ever-present throngs of devotees, Avery decamped to what she thought would be a secret location. But an Everyman from *Freaky Folks Tidings* tracked her down. She granted an interview only because she thought that by addressing her followers she would make them see she was just a regular person.

When asked her about her guru status she responded, "What do I have to teach people? I know nothing myself." The statement only made the Ponchettes think she was more profound. The article revealed the vicinity of her new studio, which was soon swarming with crowds so thick it was difficult for Avery to run simple errands or restock her supply of sage. One day, she vainly attempted to drive away the hoards by pelting them with dried apricots from an upstairs window. Shortly after that, she vanished.

The only message she left behind was spray-painted on the plaster. It was a Simon & Garfunkel lyric: "The words of the prophets are written on the subway walls." Avery's followers raced to the Astor Place stop on the 6 Train line,

crowding it beyond capacity for a few hours as they searched for a message. Finding nothing, they grew disillusioned, and soon abandoned their Ponchettes on park benches and at bus stop shelters. The boiled wool mini-capes could often be spotted the following winter as homeless men repurposed groups of three or four of them as blankets.

For a time, Avery collected her trust fund checks at a post office box in Mexico City. But it is thought she converted her fortune into gold bars or some other sort of untraceable currency.

Some fashion historians consider Avery ahead of her time, prefiguring the hybridization of "global" and "street rebel" looks made popular in the 1980s by designers such as Jean Paul Gaultier. Some even suggest that she and the Frenchman once had an encounter in Fez, although this has never been substantiated.

DRESS-IN-A-JAR

How much would you pay?

Two things invaded the bedrooms of ordinary Americans in the early 1970s: the sexual revolution and TV pitchmen, the latter of which appeared regularly on the Zenith and Sony color sets that perched on the dressers of every U.S. ranch house boudoir. Combined, these forces created Dress-in-a-Jar, a garment that was basically glorified body paint, and available only by ordering from advertisements on late-night television. It was designed to appeal to straight-laced customers who felt they had missed something by not being part of the Summer of Love five years before, people who fantasized about having "happenings" in their rec rooms, "be-ins" in their backyards, and maybe even threesomes in their two-car garages.

But the ads, which featured the garment's inventor Marilyn Roach, were not overtly sexual. They used titillation only as a subtext. On the surface, Dress-in-a-Jar was touted as practical. "Your husband will never have to help with a zipper again! How much would you pay?" a suntanned Roach enthused to the camera as she scooped an opaque, claylike substance out of a cobalt blue jar that resembled a Noxzema tub, and applied the contents to the arm of a smiling model with a shag haircut. Still photographs flashed on the screen, showing the model grocery shopping and out for a candlelit dinner, wearing what looked like a normal shift dress. Roach claimed that once on the body, her scoop-n-smear invention was barely distinguishable from a regular fabric garment.

"Long sleeves, short sleeves, no sleeves, strapless—you decide how bare to go! How much would you pay?"

But the best part of the commercial, and the one everyone talked about, was an intentionally humorous montage of how easily the dress could be removed. "So quick to take off!" Roach said in a voice-over tinged with a smoker's hoarseness,

as the model, wearing the Dress-in-a-Jar, was suddenly hit with an errant stream from a neighbor's garden hose. The frame froze just as she crossed her arms over herself and smiled, giggling, as the water began to wash away the dress and leave her standing naked on the sidewalk. This same sequence was repeated with a kitchen sink sprayer, an unexpected soak from of a sprinkler system in a public park, a tumble into a neighbor's pool, and of course a dip in a bubble bath. All of which implied that, with Dress-in-a-Jar, nudity was only seconds, or a few molecules of H_2O, away.

And how much did people pay? Only $9.99. Each jar featured a center divider separating the contents into two colors: avocado and rust. The kit came with an instruction sheet for using these shades to create stripes, polka dots, and more complicated plaid or paisley patterns.

Roach, with her frosted blonde hair and immaculate white pantsuit, looked like she might spend her spare time at a suburban country club. But she had a much shadier past. The daughter of a carny, she had a criminal record containing a series of misdemeanors and no formal training in fashion design.

The origins and formula for the spreadable dress are unclear. Some of Roach's claims could never be substantiated, such as "Adapted from a secret Swedish formula!" "Made with herbs and vitamins!" and "Worn by royalty!" But many say Roach simply got the idea from photographs of Woodstock hippies, naked except for a coating of mud, which she saw in *Time*—her favorite reading material during breaks from the off-track betting window where she worked for a short time after being released from her third stint in jail on a check forgery charge.

Dress-in-a-Jar was test-marketed in the suburbs of Gary, Indiana; Tampa, Florida; and Columbus, Ohio. "Forget playing in Peoria, it has to kill in Columbus to really make it," Roach was known to say to employees, a phrase she had lifted from her father. And kill it did. "The phones lit up, and so did my hopes for a respectable future," Roach wrote in her tell-all autobiography, *How Much I Paid*, which was never published due to laws preventing criminals from benefiting financially from their wrongdoings.

But there was a terrible flaw in the rinse-off chemise. Luckily, the fulfillment company that warehoused and shipped the goods was extremely inefficient and had only managed to get a few orders in the mail when the fault was found.

It was discovered during a Dress-in-a-Jar party at the modest Gary, Indiana, home of aspiring swingers Veronica and Howard Edgerton, held while their children were at day camp. The women milled around the kitchen, complementing each other on their Dress-in-a-Jar paisleys, and snacking on onion dip, while the men lined up along a backyard Slip 'n Slide in anticipation. Veronica was the first to begin acting strangely, claiming that bats were flying into her hair. "Green bats, smiling, with braces on their fangs," Howard Edgerton later testified. "I think that last part was because our youngest Julie had a gap in her teeth and we'd been to the orthodontist." Soon the other women were also seeing similarly surreal images.

After it was determined that this was not, in the words of party guest Arnold Smith, "some phony baloney way to chicken out," the party decamped to the emergency room, where doctors immediately diagnosed the women with having ingested some sort of strong hallucinogenic. The Edgertons had served only Chablis, dip, and chips. Since only the women were affected, Dress-in-a-Jar was thought to be the culprit. It turned out that one of the herbal ingredients had apparently fermented, creating a chemical that was so strong it was like ingesting a tab of acid.

Roach was tried in criminal court and convicted of distributing controlled substances. In a passage from *How I Much I Paid*, Roach denies any knowledge that the dresses contained potential hallucinogens. "I guess the only hallucination I had was that America would give a poor girl a fair shake." After her release from jail, Roach moved to Arizona and now owns a weight-loss spa and line of colonic products.

Disco breaks the sound barrier

1978

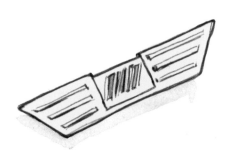

ABOVE: The red, white, and blue color palette was inspired by the French Tricolor and Air France's corresponding corporate hues. 1978.

BELOW: The string bikini was often triple-knotted to prevent mishaps on the dance floor. Anonymous. Marker sketch. 1978.

During the summer of 1978, passengers on Air France's supersonic Concorde jet traveling the New York to Paris route received a complimentary bag of travel amenities that included, among other things, a miniature bottle of Halston perfume; a crystal champagne flute designed to hold Krug Grande Cuvée (which was poured without restraint during the flight); a small "souvenir" spoon made of sterling silver, its handle encrusted with a diamond image of the Air France logo; and twelve pieces of satin lingerie with the brand name "Mach2 (by Hugo)," a reference to the speed at which the jet flew. This collection of luxury items might at first seem to be simply a celebration of the era's decadent partying spirit. But there was more to it than that.

Disco was at its peak, and the airline, at the insistence of its Hustle-addicted customers, had installed, in the aft section of the cabin, a small dance floor so tiny that it was affectionately known as "Studio 5 × 4," a play on the name of the exclusive New York discotheque. The luxury items were provided to help passengers take full advantage of this "haven of hedonism at sixty thousand feet," (as it was described on a seat-back pocket card), and also acted as somewhat of a bribe not to report the modification to the Federal Aviation Administration.

Mach2 Lingerie was the ideal airborne dance-floor wear. It replicated the often skin-baring ensembles of the disco, and on a practical level, kept traveling clothes dry and wrinkle-free—as they could remain hanging in the cabin while the wearer changed into Mach2 and worked up a sweat boogying on the tiled disco floor, which flashed red when the plane broke the sound barrier.

Of the twelve pieces in the collection, there were a few relatively modest items such as the slinky, thigh-grazing mini-slip or the bell-bottomed "lounging jumpsuit." But by the time the plane touched down in Paris most passengers on the dance floor had stripped to the string bikini top and matching panties, the jockstrap, or simply the unisex briefs.

The designer had a single name: Hugo, but that is all we know about him. Whoever he was, his creations proved more popular than any of the other amenities provided in the goody bag. They were available nowhere but the Concorde, and when worn at terrestrial discos, advertised that the wearer had reached a level of success at which supersonic jet travel was routine. Some even bought Concorde tickets just to get the Mach2. Disco crowds parted for those wearing the status lingerie. There was even a new dance called the "Hunchback Hustle," which imitated the posture of some Concorde passengers, who had to crouch over somewhat while on the Air France dance floor because the plane's ceiling was only six feet high.

Aware of the growing popularity of the Mach2, Air France offered variations on it. To honor the Paris-Dakar-Rio route, there were Carnival and road-rally themed versions. In a wink to their international passenger base, they commissioned a range of panties in colors from ivory, to olive, to cocoa brown, to blue-black, all spelling, in sequins across the rear, the word "flesh."

Although a few passengers did not appreciate the bacchanalia in the back of the plane, most did. It seemed that the era of Mach2 Lingerie would go on forever, until a fashion model passenger, who had spent much of the flight in the bathroom inspecting her souvenir spoon, was informed that the Concorde flew at twice the speed of sound. This fact puzzled her, as she did not understand why the music at "Studio 5 × 4" was playing at the same speed in the air as it would on the ground.

When no one was able to answer her question about why this was the case, she began to run about the plane in her Mach2 maillot-style bodysuit, claiming that everyone was lying to her and threatening to break the plane windows to "let in the truth." The slipperiness of her lingerie made her

ABOVE: The influence of designer Nina Ricci's 1978 Air France flight attendant uniforms can be seen in the lounging jumpsuit. Note the "AF" logo at the hem.

almost impossible to catch. She escaped the grip of everyone, vaulting over seats, climbing across laps, always crouched over somewhat in a variation of the posture used in the "Hunchback Hustle."

She was caught, thanks to the only passenger with calloused hands—a newly minted lottery winner and former machinist taking his first trip abroad. He gripped the satin fabric, snagging it enough to create the friction required to slow her down. The incident is noted in one line in the pilot's logbook. The next day, Mach2 Lingerie was deemed too dangerous to fly and grounded for good.

FUSCHETTE

Girls just want to have leggings

Fuschette was the brand name of an affordable junior line sold in regional chain stores in the New York tristate area. It began as an undistinguished collection of the era's teen trends: leggings, oversized sweatshirts, baggy tees, and minis. What made it stand out from its competitors was that it was promoted by a musical group known as Fuschette: The Band, consisting of company founder Sam Harris's thirteen-year-old daughter Lisa on vocals and lead guitar, and her two best friends, Marni on bass and Maya on drums.

The trio was modeled after the "New Wave" all-girl groups popular in the mid-1980s and played catchy songs with an upbeat tempo. Gigs included fashion trade shows, shopping mall events, church carnivals, and anywhere else Harris thought he might reach his seventh-grade customer, her parents, or the buyers who stocked the stores she patronized.

He wrote all the songs, including: "We Got the Pleats," which was based on the Go-Go's' "We Got the Beat," the original lyrics tweaked slightly to promote Fuschette's cheerleader minis made of sweatshirt fabric; "Walking in Sweatshirts," which borrowed heavily from Katrina and the Waves' "Walking on Sunshine" and celebrated the joy of strolling while wrapped in soft knitted fabric; and "Girls Just Want to Have Leggings," inspired by Cyndi Lauper's classic hit and lauding Fuschette's twenty-five colors of footless Lycra tights.

Performances lasted fifteen minutes, with Mr. Harris operating the lights and sound, and the girls wearing Fuschette outfits. The choreography was based on moves Lisa learned in Saturday morning dance classes at the neighborhood community center, and the climax was always her signature

ABOVE: Promotional drawing for Fuschette: The Band, from a trade show brochure. 1985.

series of jazz squares, done facing front and then back, so the clothing could be seen from every angle. Harris nixed any moves he considered unwholesome, and his strict standards sometimes caused friction with his daughter.

Harris insisted on an innocent yet hip image for Fuschette, and he cultivated it right down to the names of the colors, which were featured prominently on the company's heart-shaped hangtags. Each shade paired two things that evoked sweetness and purity: Strawberry Puppy, Daisy Cake, Lime Kitten, Bunny Ribbon. One mistake was the name Sun Smile. Only after the tags were printed did Harris realize that the image of yellow teeth implied decay or tobacco staining. One shade banned from Fuschette's color story was black, as Harris considered it somber and depressing.

"Daddy says Fuschette should never put anyone in a bad mood. Gag me. He's such a hypocrite," Lisa wrote in her diary, one of the many entries that betray an annoyance with her father's business tactics. The entry also reveals Lisa's frustration with her bandmates, in this case during a performance of "I'm So Coordinated," which was nearly a word-for-word copy of the Pointer Sisters' "I'm So Excited," except that it celebrated a passion for wardrobe harmonizing rather than a man. "Maya totally messed up the beat on 'Coordinated,' which messed me up on my jazz squares, so I talked to her and was nice and all, but she still, like, looked like she was going to cry."

But even though Lisa was critical, customers were not. Fuschette's price point, color range, and innocent image hit a sweet spot with the public. Sales soared. Harris hired new designers, all recent graduates from two-year fashion education programs, and had them scout trendy Manhattan boutiques for designs to reinterpret for the middle school crowd. Everything was done by calculation, not inspiration, and success followed. During Easter break, Fuschette: The Band played several venues to promote the new designs, and Lisa noticed that some of the applause was actually for the clothing.

One popular new Fuschette feature was "the fraction length," which meant that shirt sleeves and pant legs never ended at the wrist or ankle. Everything was ¾, ½, or ¼. The gimmick also saved the company money on fabric. The exception was the "⅛ sleeve," which was made of stretch jersey that had been purchased at a huge discount and could be doubled back upon itself.

"Dad totally doesn't get that for our fans, math doesn't belong in our music. They could decide to move on to the next hot thing," Lisa wrote in her diary. "I told Marni and Maya we had to confront him about it, but they totally sat there biting their lips. I don't know if they're tough enough to make it in the music business."

But despite Lisa's dire predictions, Fuschette continued to grow in popularity, and Harris extended distribution beyond the tristate area. To promote the new reach of the brand, Fuschette: The Band went on a summer tour and played at fashion shows in malls and country clubs up and down the U.S. East Coast. The schedule was grueling, but they found the time to get into the recording studio and cut a single, "Tulle Summer"—which sounded a lot like Bananarama's "Cruel Summer"—announcing Fuschette's expansion into "minicrinis" and warm-weather formalwear.

The song was pressed on colored vinyl the same shade as Fuschette's most popular hue: Strawberry Puppy. The 45 record was distributed as an insert in fashion trade magazines. By August, the group had been approached by Sire Records. Lisa wanted to sign, but Marni and Maya, tired of being ordered around by their lead singer and eager to start high school in the fall, sobbed throughout the meeting with the record executives, and then quit the band. They also stole Lisa's diary and turned it over to Mr. Harris.

Upon reading it, he decided to disband Fuschette: The Band so Lisa could focus on her studies. But she hired a lawyer and began emancipation proceedings to free herself of her parents' custody. Depositions taken in conjunction with the case show that she wanted to take Fuschette: The Band on the road, cut an entire album, and record songs about racier material. But her petition for emancipation was denied. Fuschette sold well throughout the 1980s. Four years later, Lisa went on to perform in *Cats* on Broadway.

GILDED PINSTRIPES

After hours wear for the nouveau riche

ABOVE: The Vicuna, an endangered South American grazing animal, was put at higher risk for extinction when its wool was used to make Gilded Pinstripe suits.

Only the go-go economic boom of the 1980s could have created the gilded pinstripe, also known as "status striping." Popular with a select group of nouveau riche men and women with money to burn, the stripes were fashioned from 24-karat gold thread and woven into fabric made from the world's finest wool, which was illegally shorn from the vicuna, a llama-like endangered grazing animal endemic to South America. This black-market cloth was then tailored into the era's signature "power" suit: a wide-shouldered jacket paired with fluid cuffed trousers. The opulent pinstripe, made more alluring by its criminal provenance, was must-have, after-hours wear at the exclusive new-money social clubs frequented by freshly minted Wall Street multimillionaires, global real estate barons, and Miami weapons importers.

The sole supplier and tailor of the illicit gilded pinstripe material was an expatriate Milanese Italian who had worked as an assistant at Armani, but who kept his identity secret to avoid prosecution. During fittings, he alluded to an aristocratic heritage, and joked that he was the unknown and immortal triplet brother of Romulus and Remus, the mythological twins who were said to have founded the city of Rome. His lucky customers drank Limoncello in gold-rimmed crystal glasses and gazed at the view of Central Park from his Upper East Side penthouse apartment.

Waiting lists for his services were exceedingly long. Yet today, few will admit to ever taking part in status striping because of its close association with rampant, unabated greed. Extant examples of the fabric are few: One appears in the AIDS quilt on a square for Charles Smith, a commodities trader; another in a Julian Schnabel collage-painting; and a third only in pictures, in a recently surfaced video (available on YouTube) from a 1986 Lehman Brothers Christmas party.

The holiday fete took place at the now-defunct Hamilton Club, a private Manhattan society for the freshly flush that thrived in the 1980s and hosted many of the gatherings at which the suits were worn. The little we know about gilded pinstripes comes from anecdotes shared by former Hamiltonians. These past captains of industry, many now stewards of the service sector, say the designer loved to tell the tale of how he was inspired to substitute the traditional thin white pinstripes with golden filaments. One evening at sunset, he saw a banker walking down Wall Street. The amber light bounced off her white pinstripes and turned them gold, just for a moment. "It was as if she was made of the thing she sought," the designer would say. He repeated the account ad nauseam, in his thick northern Italian accent, but he always kept secret the location of the textile mills that spun the fabric.

But there was more to the story of the gilded pinstripe, and it was passed down by Hamilton Club alumni, not because they cared about fashion history, but as a cautionary tale for anyone striving to scale the pinnacles of wealth. It was this: A feature of the suits was a quilted lining so intricate that it took on the character of a master-carved, finely detailed bas-relief. Made of ivory-colored silk that resembled polished Carrara marble (of which most of the wearers' foyers were made), these quilted interiors featured representations of heroic scenes from classical mythology: Hercules defeating the multiheaded Hydra, Odysseus crushing Trojans beneath the wheels of his chariot. These tableaux were supposed to serve as reminders to act with courage and destroy the competition. Or barring that, put on a show of bravado and cut one's losses.

Some wearers, so preoccupied with the inspiring narrative within the suit jacket, would habitually place a hand inside it and stroke the lining for comfort during difficult business negotiations—which took place as often in the smoke-filled back rooms of places like the Hamilton Club as it did boardrooms. This gesture became known by several names: "Napoleonizing," "thumb-sucking," or, in cruder terms, "yanking off Hercules," and became a "tell" of stress, fear, or weakness that, during negotiations, lost some millions.

ABOVE: The luxurious Gilded Pinstripe suit, with 24-karat gold streaks, was worn by both sexes. Contemporary artist's interpretation, based on video footage and fabric scraps.

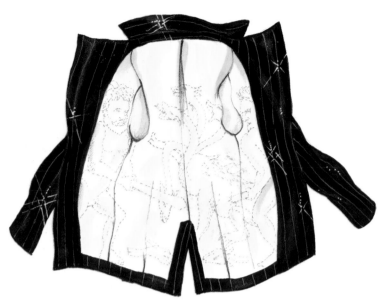

ABOVE: Gilded Pinstripe suit jacket open to show the quilted satin lining depicting Hercules slaying the Hydra. Linings showing scenes of great heroism were signature aspects of the suits.

But even without the negative effects of Napoleonizing, the garment was already destined for decline. Manufacturers of ready-to-wear suits were working on making affordable versions of gilded pinstripes, and mass availability would have killed the trend among the elite. Brooks Brothers had already produced a limited run—made in China with a much lower gold content and regular old sheep's wool—but the pieces were never brought to market. The 1987 U.S. stock market crash put a stop to ostentatious displays of wealth. The gilded pinstripe and the Milanese tailor faded away, and no one ever learned the location of the mysterious fabric mills.

For a short time in the mid-1990s there was an attempt to revive the look. A handful of Silicon Valley dot.com billionaires, who had heard about the style from Hamilton Club alumni they employed as pool boys, tried to adapt it to the technology industry. In place of gold, they planned to use copper, a tribute to the metal present in the semiconductor chips that operate modern electronics. But it turned out that producing the cloth became very expensive when done humanely; the Valleyites were shocked to learn that shearing the petite vicuna, from whose wool the original fabric had been created, often meant slaughtering it. Gathering amounts of the animal's coat small enough to preserve its life increased production costs fivefold. The endeavor was soon abandoned, and the dot.com crowd stocked up on pairs of khakis, the pale wheat color of which is sometimes referred to as "Geek Gold."

HOSPITALIA

A Japanese enfant terrible twists tradition

1987

"Taka Nakamura is so thin that it is entirely possible to believe his Parisian friends when they claim that the twenty-year-old Japanese fashion designer subsists on not much more than a daily diet of five pieces of uni sushi and one-seventh of an allotted weekly chocolate croissant. With each stride of the spindly legs that carry him from his apartment on the shabby rue de Lappe in the Bastille area to his tiny atelier in a former furniture factory, his bony knees seem dangerously close to poking holes in his tight, acid-washed jeans. His words, too, are sharp, pricking the air between us with *C'est stupide!* and *Conformiste!* in response to my questions about contemporary fashion so that I wonder, by the time we reach his studio, if his daily menu does not also include the pins that glitter from the corners of his mouth."

This is the opening paragraph of a never-published personality profile on Kyoto-born, Tokyo-trained, Paris-apprenticed enfant terrible Taka Nakamura. It was written by Michiko Saka, a young Japanese journalist living in Paris who shadowed her subject for months. The reason the piece did not run (or "was killed" in editorial lingo) was because by the time it was scheduled to print, the unorthodox designer's star had burned itself out, faster even than a fashion model's metabolism incinerates a breath mint.

Nakamura's career seemed to be on an unstoppable sky-ward trajectory after he showed his first collection in Paris. His group of dresses and tunics offered a twist on the traditional Japanese *yukata*, a simple cotton robe resembling a kimono that was typically worn after bathing or as street-wear on hot summer nights. In Nakamura's hands, it became something one would don for the most avant-garde of parties. Where usual *yukata* patterns were quite benign—koi fish or fans

ABOVE: Nakamura preferred provocative fabric patterns. Here, skulls and mushroom clouds; evil Uncle Sams. 1987.

OPPOSITE: Design drawing for the *yukata*-inspired Hospitalia collection. Note the pattern of flaming dollar signs. Taka Nakamura. Marker. 1987.

rendered in white and indigo, florals or kites done in pastels—Nakamura aimed to shock. He used the same colorways, but created fabric that displayed imagery critical of the Cold War and capitalism: skeletons and mushroom clouds; devil-like Uncle Sams and flaming dollar signs made of snakes.

But even more unusual was the modified silhouette, which ignored the shape of the body beneath, and became somewhat like wearable sculpture. Like regular *yukatas*, Nakamura's were wraparounds that tied with a sash, but he had treated the fabric so the surface texture was permanently crinkled and twisted and so stiff that the garments stood away from the wearer so it looked as if he or she had been hit by a gust of wind. One critic compared the neo-*yukatas* to tangled sheets, and called the runway models "a bunch of walking sickbeds." This earned the collection the nickname "Hospitalia." Others whispered quietly that the mannequins looked struck by a nuclear blast.

Even with these negative connotations, a small but influential crowd of fashion-forward customers embraced the Nakamura *yukata*. The core group was acquainted because their grandparents had been patrons of the surrealist Salvador Dali and met monthly at each other's apartments to admire the impromptu murals the artist had painted on various living room walls during raucous 1920s parties.

The fact that, from Nakamura's waiflike form were frequently issued powerfully barbed remarks, was balm to these preservationists of surrealism who, naturally, swooned over unexpected juxtapositions. The designer became an instant fixture at their fetes and could often be seen "in front of a mural of a giant eyeball, much of the black iris having flaked away, raging about the sameness of everything. His skin is as pale as a squid's belly, his hair as black as the ink the undersea animal sprays to ward off predators. He informs his own Hospitalia–clad clients that they dress, think, and act so uniformly that he cannot tell them apart. But rather than take offense, they are enchanted, and simply nod. Yet his thorniness is not as sharp here as on the rue de Lappe. The lush carpets and bergère chairs seem to absorb some of it. It threatens to become part of the décor."

And that is exactly what happened. It was not long before the women who wore Nakamura's designs began to copy the bad boy himself. They dieted to make their already slight frames even more gaunt, wore acid-washed jeans under their Hospitalia *yukatas*, accused everyone of being a *Conformiste!*, and dyed their hair black, cutting it in Nakamura's "asymmetrical style, so severe that from one side he appears to have been shorn for a businessman's luncheon and on the other coiffed for a rock star dinner." The mealtime metaphors were prescient. For with his growing popularity, Nakamura began to eat.

It was only one of the changes he made to his daily routine. As his clients became his clones, simply to be himself was to be a dreaded *conformiste*. Terrified of turning into what he despised, he altered everything. Instead of one-seventh of a chocolate croissant, he had seven entire pastries. Rather than a few pieces of uni sushi, he had steak and pommes frites. He shaved his head. He lay in the sun on his rooftop and grew very tan. His demeanor became soft, even gentle. The sketches for his next collection show draped cashmere *yukatas* made from traditionally snow-dyed white yarn, with appliqués of doves and embracing couples.

But these were never to be produced, for the final alteration Nakamura made was to give up fashion design altogether. He closed his atelier and stopped attending parties. His clients asked each other what had become of him, not realizing that they saw him every day: a portly suntanned bald man with a smile on his face, ambling through the Marais. His stylish former selves passed him on the street in their neo-*yukatas*, running their pale hands through their asymmetrical black cuts, and frowning at how much space he took up on the sidewalk.

Whether Nakamura was a true nonconformist, a compulsive individualist, or a simple reactionary has been debated. He eventually quit Paris, leaving no forwarding address. Some say he used his newfound physical bulk for social protest: blocking the entrances to nuclear power plants during demonstrations. Others claim he utilized his massive form to comfort children by playing Santa Claus at orphanages around the world—although he insisted on doing it any day of the year, not just Christmas.

BONSAI DRESS (LLBD)

The littlest little black dress, ever

The Bonsai Dress, also known as the "littlest little black dress" (LLBD) ever, was the ultimate in early-1990s minimalism. Named for "bonsai," the arboreal art of cultivating miniature trees by vigorous pruning—the garment had a similarly pared-down aesthetic. It was made of a patented Lycra-like microfiber and weighed just one ounce. When not in use, it could be rolled into a marble-sized ball and tossed in a purse. Yet when worn, the seemingly magical material smoothed even the most egregious figure flaws while creating a timeless silhouette. This made it not only small in size but tiny-to-invisible as a source of anxiety for the wearer.

In sum, it was the perfect little black dress: flattering, chic, always at the ready—a sort of "Holy Grail" of LBDs. At least, in theory. And in theory it will always remain, as the Bonsai, for reasons soon to be explained, was never actually seen by the public or even the fashion press.

A promising yet vague vision of it, including the characteristics described above, was first conjured publicly by its creators, the team of Antonio LaRocca, an Italian fashion designer, and Berndt Braun, a German chemical engineer, in a brief interview in a July 1992 issue of *Women's Wear Daily*. LaRocca reported, "We chose the name 'Bonsai' because we are creating a small-scale version of a classic." Braun explained that he had originally developed the fabric, called Super-Stretch, to make winter gloves for autobahn maintenance workers. But the pair declined to go into specifics, such as hemline, neckline, or sleeve-length, saying only, "Our collection will show nineteen variations of the style, and all of them will be the most perfect dress you have ever seen."

As soon as news of the Bonsai hit print, rumors about the diminutive garment spread through the fashion community. The "LLBD" nickname is said to have been coined by an acronym-loving design assistant who was working to create new fonts for monograms at Tommy Hilfiger. The usually jaded group of fashion insiders—designers, editors, photographers, store buyers—was for some reason taken with the idea of the minute invention.

It was said that the dress was so lightweight, it was as comfortable as wearing a shadow. That it took off at least ten pounds, more if you needed it. Americans believed that it would enhance the bustline, Brazilians that it would lift the rear end, the French that it would nip in the waist, the British that it would make them more clever. Some gossips claimed that the LLBD had been worn for years by the most elite and beautiful women in the world—that they even slept in it—as the fibers helped preserve their youth.

All the speculation fueled an increasing obsession with the Bonsai. Photographs purporting to be of the dress were released by anonymous sources. The images, never commented upon by LaRocca and Braun, were viewed, deconstructed, and debunked by those in fashion's innermost circles, who were suddenly displaying the truth-seeking fervor of UFO enthusiasts. Las Vegas oddsmakers took bets on who would be the first woman to be photographed in the LLBD and how much the dress would actually weigh.

Many said it would become as iconic as a Chanel knit suit and waited breathlessly for its debut, which was to occur in New York during the September fashion shows.

The Bonsai's coming-out party took place on a terrace overlooking Central Park East that opened from the palatial apartment of a wealthy patron of LaRocca and Braun's. When the day finally arrived, all the top names in fashion were there. Some brought magnifying glasses or binoculars, just to be prepared in the case the LLBD was smaller than imagined.

Sprays of black orchids and rented bonsai trees lined the terrace, where guests sat in white folding chairs on either side of a runway topped with black onyx tile. Magnums of champagne poked from ice buckets, and there was plenty of opportunity to sample the bubbly, as the show's start time came and went without even the slightest peep from the designers. LaRocca and Braun were assumed to be behind the tower-

RIGHT: Bonsai Dress. Note the model's similarity to supermodel Cindy Crawford. 1992.

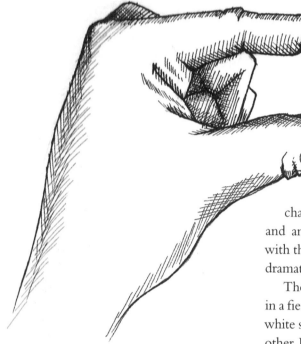

ABOVE: Bonsai Dress. Actual size when not worn.

ing white screens that had been set up at one end of the runway to create a backstage area in which to dress the models, who would appear in the promised nineteen variations of the Bonsai.

As many attendees later reported, the guests did not seem to mind the wait. It was a particularly warm evening for September, and they were chatting amicably, their excitement-flushed complexions and animated conversations becoming increasingly in sync with the early evening sky, which grew both pinker and more dramatic as sunset neared.

Then, just as the sun was dipping behind the autumn trees in a fiery burst of orange, there suddenly came, from behind the white screens, the most terrific bang. And then another, and another. Reports from those present say that it was obviously not gunshots, yet some fashionistas ducked under their chairs anyway. Others began to scream. And almost everyone later reported that they felt as if they were being stung by bees.

But the smarting pinpricks of pain were not caused by a swarm of pollinating insects but flying pieces of the Bonsai dresses. Backstage, as dressers helped models shimmy into the collection of nineteen perfect Bonsais, the Super-Stretch fabric, after hours of exposure to the afternoon sun (a stress test Braun had not thought to perform in the lab), was heated to such a point that it was unable to withstand the increased surface tension caused by expanding over even waiflike bodies. It snapped—causing each dress to explode into tiny pieces. The fashion shrapnel had a powerful initial trajectory, shooting over or through the white curtains and into the crowd, and although no one was seriously injured (the dressers managed to dive out of the way), the incident was still quite startling.

The fragments landed in the hair of some of the top supermodels of the time. One stuck to Linda Evangelista's left cheek, and that night led Cindy Crawford to accuse her of copying her signature beauty mark. Another adhered to the lens of fashion photographer Mario Testino, rendering his pictures of the fray unusable—a fate that befell all the other shooters present as well. A particularly mischievous scrap hit

Vogue editor-in-chief Anna Wintour's right buttock, which she mistook for a pinch. She turn around and slapped the nearest likely culprit, who happened to be Suzy Menkes, fashion editor of the *International Herald Tribune*.

The next day, some style-watchers called the explosion a metaphor for fashion designers who try to go too big, too soon. Others rolled their eyes and phoned Las Vegas to get their money back.

Pieces of the LLBD were found as far away as the Central Park Zoo across the street. One shred even became entangled in the works of the Zoo's famous whimsical Delacorte Musical Clock, which plays nursery rhymes on the half hour as bronze statues of animals circle about on top of a brick arcade. We know this because of an article in *The New Yorker*'s "Talk of the Town" section entitled "Big Ben" that follows a day in the life of a repairman who specializes in fixing oversized outdoor timepieces—and whose name happens to match the moniker given to the massive clock outside London's Houses of Parliament.

"Ben reached the tweezers beneath the bronzed bear's left foot and extirpated a shred of something black. He held it out so I could see. It was a piece of fabric. Attached was the kind of white tag one might find inside a shirt collar. It read: 'Bonsai.' 'That's a small thing ain't it? A bonsai,' Ben said. 'To mess up something so big.' He looked up at the sky, which he calls his 'clock without hands,' placed the offending shred carefully in his trash bag and chimed, 'Lunch.'"

And what of Antonio LaRocca and Berndt Braun? To the disappointment of their patron and other investors, they fled Manhattan soon after the fashion show, heavily in debt. No one has seen them since.

Counterfeit Superstar sneakers

The counterfeiting of name-brand fashion goods became part of the style landscape in the 1990s. One bogus item was the Adididas, a phony version of the Adidas Superstar sneaker. It was identifiable as inauthentic most obviously by the surplus "di" syllable in the brand name that appeared on the tongue and heel, but also because it had six stripes instead of three, a "trefoil" logo that looked like a smashed cockroach, and a classic "shell toe" covering that appeared to be made of wax. Produced at an unknown location somewhere in Greece, it was sold by North African immigrants on the streets of Europe.

Adididas quickly became stylish with carefree, European-capital-hopping backpacking youth, who found the shoes laugh-out-loud hilarious. The footwear's egregious flaws made them more entertaining and better-selling than more accurate counterfeits. Adididas were so far from the original that they had their own identity.

It became stylish not only to wear Adididas, but to dangle an extra pair from the edge of one's backpack. Many trekkers around Europe that summer wandered the observation deck at the top of the Eiffel Tower accompanied by the dull thud of the rubberized soles slapping together. This same sound was a counterpoint to the songs of the Venice gondoliers and the military band at the Changing the Guard at Buckingham Palace.

The Adididas were made of inferior leather, or perhaps vinyl, although sometimes they seemed to be constructed of discarded car headliners, old tires, or shredded patio furniture. Each new batch was different, and as the summer progressed, word would spread throughout the youth hostels whenever a new version of the tragic failure called Adididas arrived for sale on the streets. The news was treated much as Fendi fans would greet the bulletin that a limited-edition Spy handbag

ABOVE: Versions of the Adidas trefoil logo as it appeared on the Adididas counterfeit shoe. Pencil. 1995.

had hit the stores—with a buying frenzy. Crowds pushed and shoved to purchase the new pairs of Adididas that were lined up neatly on the white sheets lain on the cobblestones by men from Morocco and Ethiopia.

The men who sold the shoes handed them over with wide smiles and assurances of authenticity. The most common phrase they used was: "This is real," which ran together and was pronounced like one word that sounded like: "Thesisreal." "Thesisreal" became a code word among backpackers for one-night love, a lighthearted euphemism college students from different countries would laughingly whisper to each other before sharing a passionate encounter on a ferry crossing the Aegean Sea, making clear that there were no expectations of commitment.

The Adididas, too, could often end up as a quickie affair. Sometimes an Adididas disintegrated after only a few days, especially in places with extremely polluted air such as Athens, where after just minutes, the shoes simply became white dust clouds that hovered around the feet for a moment before blowing away to join the mass of particulate matter devouring the temples on the Acropolis. Adididas were unpredictable, too. One pair might be impervious to water, while another fell apart seconds after the wearer stepped in a puddle. Sometimes an Adididas would be complete in the morning, when leaving a hostel, campsite, pension, or two-star hotel, but by noon a hole would appear in the toe, or a stripe would peel away.

The laces, too, were made of mysterious and varying materials that sometimes smelled of gasoline, other times feet, or a dentist's office. Once, a group of Germans doing their gap year and drunk on Jägermeister used a fish-smelling Adididas lace to flavor a stew, bay leaf style, and for days afterwards reported they felt a heightened sense of invincibility.

Some mischievous backpackers had Adididas Olympics, with competitions to see how long it would take to destroy the shoe. They threw it against the wall, where some Adididas exploded

The only known images of the Adididas come from the Moleskine notebook of an art student traveling in Europe in the summer of 1995. Among sketches of grand artistic and architectural landmarks, such as the fountain seen **ABOVE**, are scattered depictions of various versions of the counterfeit shoe. The drawing **BELOW** shows one that was abandoned on the steps of the Louvre. Note the stripes peeling away from the side and the "Adididas" spelling on the heel.

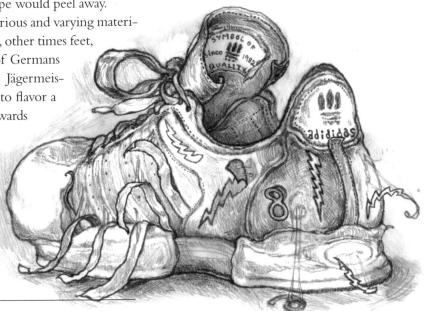

immediately like firecrackers. They ran down cobblestone streets and after a single block, compared holes in the soles to see whose sock had the most visible surface area. They sat in the sun at sidewalk cafes, with their feet propped up, and timed how quickly the stripes peeled away and fell to the ground like leaves as the adhesive failed in the afternoon heat. They licked gelato at town square fountains and argued about who was the winner as the spray of water caused some Adididas to turn black and wither, while others bubbled and sizzled.

Some meaner backpackers (often Australians) played a harsher game. Having learned the word for "police" in nearly every language, they chased the sellers of Adididas through the streets, warning them of the approach of nonexistent law enforcement officers. The North Africans quickly folded their sheets around the Adididas, making giant bundles, and fled like so many Santa Clauses, often losing an Adididas in the process.

Perhaps a desire to punish those who played this game was behind one of the many superstitions that sprang up around Adididas. The most famous was the Curse of the Lonely Adididas. If you saw an Adididas by itself—sitting in a gutter, floating in a canal, wherever—when you were also alone, you would never marry. The only way to counteract this was to pick up the solo Adididas, take it to a bar, ask for it to be filled up with tap-drawn beer, and guzzle the entire contents. This was especially popular with soccer hooligans.

Then one day the Adididas got better. The logo on the side looked less like a pot leaf, or a screaming man with his hair on fire, or a glove for someone with no pinky or thumb. The air vents were actually punched all the way through instead of drawn on top with a ballpoint pen. The shell toe was made of rubber. The sole's thickness was consistent, whereas before it had always seemed like the ball or heel of the foot had been melted in a fire.

As a success, the Adididas were a failure, at least with the backpackers. They stopped buying them. For their trekking customers, the North African salesmen soon replaced them with another product from the same supplier: purses by Louis Vuittonton.

BELOW: Counterfeit Adidas Superstar after exposure to water spray from the Trevi Fountain in Rome. Note the violent sizzling. Pencil. 1995.

TRIFLING COAT

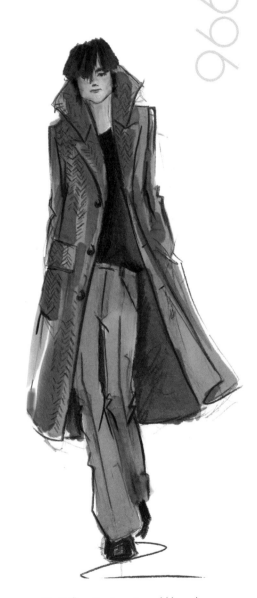

The Trifling Coat first gained popularity at a Los Angeles coffee shop called Paradox, where young men who aspired to be staff writers on television situation comedies spent entire days trading sardonic witticisms over their laptops. Many of them were swaddled in the three-quarter length overcoat, which was constructed of ultra-lightweight wool. Nearly sheer, it was comfortable even in L.A.'s year-round summertime temperatures, yet the herringbone pattern, leather-wrapped buttons, and notched lapel collar—worn turned up as if to protect against the cold—gave it a wintry air. In a city sans windchill or blizzards, it was the ultimate ironic outerwear—ideal for those who insisted they took nothing seriously, and wanted everyone to know it.

But humor had been the furthest thing from the mind of the coat's original creator, a Hollywood wardrobe mistress named Jennifer Reese. On set, it had pained her to see that outerwear-clad "extras" (or "background") in film and television often fainted during exterior scenes shot in the scorching L.A. sun. She herself had performed CPR on a female "extra" who had lain unconscious and unnoticed, swathed in a ten-pound camel hair coat, under a pile of fake snow in ninety-degree heat on the Warner Bros. lot's "New York Street" during the filming of a Christmas episode of *Everybody Loves Raymond*.

The woman survived, but the incident gave Reese, who had trained in Paris, the inspiration for what she called the "Trompe l'Audience," or "fool the audience" coat. With the look of heavy tweed, but without the weight, the Trompe was intended to keep day-players cool and viewers securely behind the fourth wall. She made twenty samples, sourcing the fabric from cheap mills to ensure its thinness, and creating styles that represented a range of historical eras. But not

ABOVE: The Trifling Coat, as it would have been worn by an aspiring sitcom writer. *Los Angeles Magazine*. Anonymous. November, 1996.

ABOVE: Designer Jennifer Reese's presentation sketch for the Trifling Coat when it was still known as the *Trompe L'Audience*. Marker. 1996.

OPPOSITE: Two sketches for the original *Trompe L'Audience* coat, which was designed to make the working lives of Hollywood extras more bearable. Jennifer Reese. Marker. 1996.

one costume supervisor or studio executive would even meet with her to look at them.

We know all of this because Reese appeared in a reality TV program pilot called *Ent-REAL-preneurs*, which tracked the efforts of several individuals starting their own businesses. The show was never picked up by a network.

In *Ent-REAL-preneur* footage from a blind date Reese went on with a line producer, her companion makes clear the reason for the industry's lack of interest in the Trompe. As the two sip margaritas at a Mexican restaurant called El Coyote, he laughingly tells her no studio would be interested in wasting budget money on purchasing the Trompe, as extras are easy to come by, and any lost, even permanently, through dehydration can be easily replaced.

In a post-date face-to-face with the camera Reese says: "He told me if I was such a humanitarian I should move out of L.A. and go work for UNICEF."

Discouraged, Reese distributed the Trompe to a few friends. But in Hollywood, there is a deeply held belief that failure is contagious, and the coats were discarded as if they were smallpox-laden blankets. Footage from *Ent-REAL-preneurs* shows Reese's friends selling the coats to a vintage clothing shop on Melrose Avenue. The store was within a slow amble from Paradox, so it can be assumed that this is how the garments were discovered by the aspiring sitcom writers.

The missing piece is how the coat that began with such earnest, high-minded intentions ended up being nicknamed the Trifling Coat. A clue comes from a *Los Angeles Magazine* article, "Espresso Yourself: What Your Coffee Drink Says About You," one of the publication's occasional humorous roundups that helped readers identify their personal L.A. "type" by a whimsical classification system. One of these was the "Triple-Shot Trifler," a "witty, wired comic scribe most often spotted at Paradox."

Local fashion design students noted the coat's popularity as an icon for the ironic and soon began making copies to sell at low-end Melrose Avenue boutiques. Trifling Coats became favored attire at L.A. game nights, karaoke outings, and improvisational comedy festivals. One or two may have even been purchased by professional day-players.

The closest the Trifling Coat came to an on-screen dramatic appearance was in the only episode of *Friends* that never aired: "The One Where Chandler Writes." In front of the live audience, the scenes of Matthew Perry pecking at a keyboard in a funny-looking overcoat fell flat. A friend of Reese's who worked on the show told her about the Trompe's appearance, but, unwilling to make waves, she simply pretended it had never happened.

Even if Reese had claimed some sort of ownership of the Trifling Coat's design, she could not have stopped its decline in popularity. With the growing number of reality programs on television, many hopeful sitcom writers gave up their dreams of penning the next great pilot. They traded the mocking overcoats for sweatshirts, the requisite uniform for Hollywood production assistants. They were still seen at Paradox, most often placing large orders for custom coffee drinks to take back to the staff at the offices in which they worked.

Perhaps the best way to sum up the trend would be with another excerpt from the footage of Reese's post-date, face-to-face with the camera on *Ent*-REAL-*preneurs*: "I just wanted to make something that would help the people who never really get lucky in this town, you know?" In one of the many ironies in the story of a garment laden with irony, she did just that—temporarily, of course, and not in the way she had intended.

EMOTIONALLY DISTRESSED JEANS

The brainchild of business and psychology

ABOVE: Image from rare promotional postcard (one of only one hundred hand-delivered to a select client list) announcing Emotionally Distressed Jeans in the "Amanda" (or "Heartbreak") style. Anonymous. 1998.

Displayed between two sheets of Plexiglas in an ultramodern Tokyo penthouse apartment is one of the world's rarest pairs of blue jeans, preserved with the care usually reserved for an antique kimono. Like many late-1990s indigos, the pair is artificially distressed: faded, torn, and whiskered. Yet it was not created by a high-end denim designer, but a depressed, freshman girl at an American university. It was a product of the Emotionally Distressed Jeans project, an exclusive line available only on the black market to an elite group of extremely wealthy consumers.

The jeans were the brainchild of a secret partnership between two groups of graduate students—psychology and business—at the University of Pennsylvania. They believed that negative emotions, instead of being quashed with the decade's drug of choice, Prozac, should be expressed and channeled into lucrative endeavors. Unbeknownst to UPenn administrators, they tested this out by giving a fresh pair of stiff indigo jeans to every student who visited the school's mental health counseling center. The recipients were instructed to take out all their frustration and anxiety on the denim—rather than themselves or their friends—for a week. Seven days later, the "emotionally distressed" jeans were returned to the center, along with a logbook listing the methods used to create the damages.

The psychology students' field notes show the distressers reported an improved sense of well-being and elevated self-esteem. With each pair of returned jeans, the MBA-seekers had a template from which they manufactured a limited-edition series of denims, named after the individual distresser and selling for a profit of five thousand dollars each, an amount they split with their psych grad partners. The jeans were advertised only through word of mouth, and seven styles stood out as highly popular.

The model most in demand with rich rock musicians was the "Amanda" or "Heartbreak" jean, created by a waiflike art major of the same name. The low-rise flare was hand-abraded with items left behind in her dorm room by a cheating musician boyfriend: a guitar pick, a Green Day CD, and steel guitar strings. Fraying at the hem was achieved by repeatedly slamming the jeans against a cinderblock wall. They had a special key pocket to store the spurned lover's tool of choice for vandalizing an ex's car.

The "Jennifer" was a privileged jean with a secret story to tell. An elegant dark denim wash, with a conservative eight-inch rise, tailored fit, and boot cut, the only signs of damage were several thin white scrapes across the thighs created with a Mont Blanc pen. But inside, in tight block letters, was written the story of every disappointment, social slight, and moment of sadness familiar to any advantaged eighteen-year-old. This model was a sellout in socialite circles.

The bipolar "Melissa" was a free-spirited bell-bottom with a faded wash and sharp creases down the front. It could easily go from day to night, office to dance club, or elation to hopelessness. The knee tears were the result of activities brought on by moments of manic ecstasy, such as jumping over barbed wire fences or climbing apple trees, while the creases were achieved through hours of somber pressing. Hollywood starlets adored the "Melissa."

International guy-candy models clamored for the "Jason," an obsessive-compulsive, cigarette-leg denim available in waist sizes of twenty-seven inches or less and washed over thirty-seven times in the UPenn dorm community laundry facility.

The mottled "dirty wash" of the ultra low-slung "Jessica" benefited from an attention deficit to details. One leg was soaked in a mud puddle, while the other was abraded by tire tracks that overlapped numerous times to form an abstract pattern.

Young Wall Street retirees formed a waiting list for the relaxed-fit, 100 percent cotton "Josh," which got its trademark bohemian rumpled look from being rolled into a ball, hand-drizzled with candle wax, soaked with water from automatic dorm fire sprinklers, then bound with twine and kicked up

ABOVE: "Amanda," art student creator of "Heartbreak" jean. Image was not a portrait, but an invented likeness to protect her privacy. From promotional postcard. Anonymous. 1998.

BELOW: Tools used to distress the "Amanda" jean: guitar pick, steel guitar string, and case for Green Day's *Nimrod* CD. The tracks "Platypus (I Hate You)" and "Take Back" were heard coming from the designer's dorm room while she distressed the jeans. From promotional postcard. Anonymous. 1998.

and down the halls of the Philosophy department like a soccer ball.

Finally, there was the "Lenny," created by a tenure-track English professor and beloved for its melancholy post-1960s vibe. Bleached to a yellow-white that suggested the pages of a long-unpublished manuscript, the embroidered detailing on the back pocket included a rainbow peace sign shredded to an almost unrecognizable state.

The Emotionally Distressed Jeans project came to a halt when one of the grad students' regular customers, a Finnish glam metal guitarist, insisted on having a pair of denims created by what he termed a "certifiable psychotic." These patients were beyond the treatment means of the UPenn student mental health center. One of the business school students, determined to provide the utmost in customer service, tried to sneak a pair of fresh indigos into the state psychiatric care facility, hoping to find a patient willing to distress them. He was caught by police and, during questioning, the secret program was exposed. It was quickly stopped by UPenn administrators, who thoroughly hushed it up.

The jeans are still valuable to collectors, who buy and sell them through private channels. The Japanese billionaire who displays the "Amanda" in his living room overlooking Tokyo Bay reportedly paid 250,000 dollars for them. And for those who consider the Emotionally Distressed Jeans project exploitative, records show that after it was discontinued, students at the counseling center reported resurgences of depression, and referrals for Prozac prescriptions jumped 35 percent.

BERTRAND DESPAIR GLOVE

Gauntlet for a grim world

2002

Bicycle messengers in industrialized cities from Chicago to Shanghai started this trend when they began duct-taping travel packs of Kleenex onto the backs of their riding gloves. This allowed them to conveniently blot away smog-induced tears without having to sacrifice efficiency by slowing down. The "tape-n-tissue" practice was soon copied by certain pedestrians in the Western world, but not for the purpose of pollution absorption. The adapters were typically sensitive adolescents, or "Emo" kids. They often suffered unpredictable sobbing episodes brought on by sudden reminders of the state of the world (which they considered quite grim) and needed a way to dry their eyes without having to stop and risk missing the bus that took them to art school.

The look hit the mainstream at fall/winter Paris Fashion Week, when it was adapted for the debut collection of Adèle Bertrand, a nineteen-year-old, self-taught designer and daughter of a minor *Les Verts* party politician and a neo-Bauhaus architect. She accessorized her highly structured PVC dresses and suits with Teflon-coated elbow-length gloves that resembled those used for motorcycle racing, but on the backs of the hands she added quilted oval patches in quick-dry, wick-away fabric. Bertrand called them "Despair Gloves."

By all accounts, the runway show was stunning. Models entered with thick black tears running down their cheeks, blotting them with the gloves as they strutted to a soundtrack of Joy Division's 1981 album *Still* and a slide show of war-torn landscapes. At the finale, the models took the usual en masse turn, but then collapsed, sobbing into the gauntlets, and stayed on the catwalk. Soon it became clear they were not going anywhere. Fashion editors, celebrities, and other guests grew increasingly uncomfortable and finally filed out to what

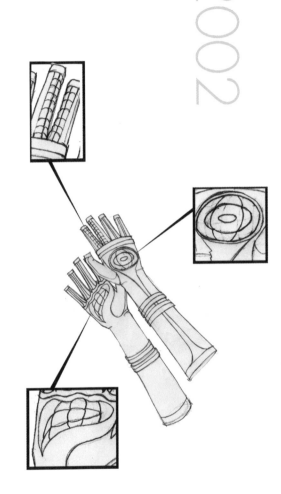

ABOVE: Bertrand Despair Glove, with close ups of the quilted oval patch in quick-dry, wick-away fabric for blotting tears; a palm grip inspired by bicycle gloves; and finger armor. Adèle Bertrand. Pencil. 2002.

Three PVC dresses from Adèle Bertrand's collection, accessorized with Despair Gloves. A plan to customize the gloves by including an embroidered letter denoting the wearer's blood type was abandoned. Design sketch. Adèle Bertrand. Marker. 2002.

some bloggers reported was the "sound of hiccups, the repeated dirgelike melody of 'Walked in Line' and a projected image of twisted metal."

There was much discussion in the fashion press about whether the tears were genuine. Some accused Bertrand of placing irritants in the mascara. Others said the models were suffering from authentic unhappiness, champagne having been banned backstage. Style.com called the spectacle "a tasteless, saltwater stained love letter to negativism" and, in a rare move, took down the video of the show from their Web site.

Of all the major department store buyers, only those from Barneys ordered the Bertrand Despair Glove, and only for their flagship Manhattan store. But they soon realized their mistake. Store managers reported that display cases were smashed by the unlikely partnership of bike messengers and Emo kids who claimed the Paris designer had co-opted their ideas. The messengers demanded financial compensation; the Emos just wanted to be heard. Bertrand accused the store of fabricating the vandalism story and using it as an excuse to send back the gloves for returns. Litigation is pending.

An aftereffect of the trend was the formation of "the broken-wing Mercuries," a small group of Emo kids who became bike messengers. They intentionally stop, often blocking traffic, to wipe the grit of progress from their eyes.

HOOD-OLO

A botched "hoodie" goes couture

In this modification of the popular "hoodie" sweatshirt, the entire jacket segment was done away with, leaving only an oversized head covering so big that it was cinched with a drawstring at the hips. Especially popular with young people in Queens, New York; the outer suburbs of Paris; London Council flats; and Tokyo, the Hood-olo was the result of a botched batch of regular sweatshirts. The seamstresses at an Indonesian factory were given sewing instructions in English, which were translated incorrectly by a foreman. The "hood-onlys," as the results were quickly dubbed, were shipped worldwide to discount shops specializing in defective merchandise, where they were sold alongside plastic water pitchers with backward spouts and chocolate bars with nougat on the outside.

One of these stores, Scotland's sprawling Product Land, located in the suburbs of Glasgow, was particularly influential in turning the look into a global trend. The store had been immortalized in the graphic novels of reclusive cult writer and artist Dutton Sinclair. In his works, Product Land was the locus of a dystopian near-future world where his characters worked, shopped, socialized, and met to plan a rebellion against an oppressive oligarchy, known as the "Prags" (short for pragmatists). In real life, the Product Land aisles were popular with teenagers engaged in role-playing games that re-enacted the activities of Sinclair's characters.

When the teens discovered the garment, they were enchanted by its somewhat monk-like, medieval look, and it became part of their games. They wore it while staging harmless showdowns in the aisles, armed with Product Land offerings such as spatulas made from aluminum foil rather than aluminum; bubble gum carving knives; and triggerless water

ABOVE: Hood-olo character by graphic novelist Dutton Sinclair. Based on sketches he did of Scottish teenagers.

pistols. They took pictures of their Product Land exploits and beamed them around the world through MySpace pages and in chat rooms dedicated to the fans of Dutton Sinclair. Other teens saw them and sought out the defective hoodie at local discount stores, or created homemade copies.

It should be noted that Product Land was also where the garment gained the name by which it became known. While using the touch-type system to enter the data for the "hood-only" sales tag into the store computer, an underpaid qwerty-keyboard operating stockroom worker had a sudden arthritic spasm in her right index finger, making her unable to stretch the digit at the angle required to reach the "n" and "y" keys, leaving only "hood-olo.")

The Hood-olo came in university-esque colors such as crimson, gold, and royal blue. After one washing, the cotton faded to a mottled finish. Hood-olos were often combined with other flawed garments found at discount stores: thermal undershirts made from waffle-weave fabric consisting not of the traditional small insular squares, but ones measuring 4×4, the result of malfunctioning textile software somewhere in China. There were one-armed T-shirts; two-thumbed mittens; three-legged carpenter pants; four-piece bikinis; fishing vests accidentally implanted with chips designed to be embedded in greeting cards so they played music when opened; wrap dresses that only went halfway around; and boots whose lug soles happened to form a pattern that left behind footprints that spelled out curse words.

Even for those not interested in Sinclair's work, the Hood-olo held appeal. Chaboards reveal teens liked that it was capacious enough to accommodate a backpack or even another person. But because it was the chosen garb of young people, a moral panic sprang up about the Hood-olo. Of the many social ills that were quickly attributed to it by pundits and preachers, one was that it created a fabric cave where illicit activities could take place. Around the world, parents shut down their children's laptops, confiscated their Hood-olos, and accused them of a multitude of sins. The boys and girls stared, wide-eyed, disbelieving that their parents thought so little of them. Brokenhearted, they left home and huddled

BELOW AND OPPOSITE: variations of the Hood-olo seen on runways in New York, London, Paris, and Milan. *W Magazine.* 2005.

FORGOTTEN FASHION

together on stoops and in drainage tunnels, in subway stations and playgrounds.

Many posted online that they felt as misunderstood as the Dutton Sinclair character, the Candle of Gonwyn, a floating cylinder of light made of pure goodness that sometimes showed other characters the way toward love, or an escape to safety. In Sinclair's stories, the Candle was vilified by the Prag oligarchy for its physical insubstantiality and refusal to serve humankind in a more practical and productive manner, such as lighting a factory floor.

The authorities blamed the Hood-olos, rather than parents, for driving children to run away from home—it was thought the generous amount of fabric made it less of a hardship to "sleep out."

At this news, Dutton Sinclair finally got involved, coming to the defense of his fans in his own way by creating an entire herd of new characters called Hood-olos. Their job was to

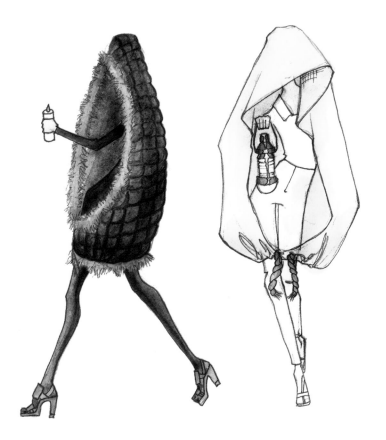

protect the Candle of Gonwyn when it was in danger of being snuffed out by the Prags. They did this by surrounding the Candle, the Hood-olos blocking the light emanating from it, so the Candle would be safely hidden.

The publicity caused by all of this caught the interest of videogame producers, who paid the suddenly famous Dutton Sinclair record sums of money to create a version of his graphic novels for the homevideo market. Buzz about the deal led to increased mentions in the media, which expanded to include even more coverage of the persecution of the real-life teen Hood-olo wearers. Soon, reporters were chastising police and parents for "profiling" and stereotyping. Human rights groups threatened a lawsuit. And the din faded away.

Like all fashions initially considered dangerous, the Hood-olo was eventually incorporated into several designer ready-to-wear collections. In Paris, it was done in quilted black satin with chinchilla trim and a velvet drawstring, with the model marching down the runway with a single white electric pillar candle. London showed it in billowing Indian cotton with a bleached rope tie, the mannequin holding a brass ship's lantern. In Milan, it was gold lamé lined in sheared mink, cinched with a gold chain and illuminated by a gilded candelabrum. The New York variation was suede lined in fleece and tied with a leather cord, with the model holding a flashlight. Yet with all of these variations on a theme, it never sold well and the silhouette was abandoned by the fashion world the following season.

ILLUSTRATORS

DENA BLANKMEYER, a 2008 Valedictorian graduate of the esteemed Fashion Institute of Design and Merchandising, has many awards to her credit, including Artist of the Year, and was the inaugural winner of the Robert Fisher Scholarship. In addition to illustration, her work includes original fashion designs, commissioned paintings, and specialty tutoring. 1905 BODY MUFF, 1964 CASSIDY TROUSER SUIT, 1972 DRESS-IN-A-JAR

TERI CHUNG was born and raised in Seoul, Korea and relocated to New York City in her late teens. She earned her BFA in Illustration from Parsons School of Design in 2003 and got her first job at the Donna Karan Company, which opened her eyes to the fashion industry. Currently, she is a fashion/graphic designer at PRPS and a freelance illustrator. 1907 TICKER TAPE TRIM, 1916 PICASSO PATCHWORK, 1923 ROBE DE CHAMPAGNE, 1970 PONCHETTES, 1998 EMOTIONALLY DISTRESSED JEANS

ELIZABETH DRAN is a recent graduate of Parson's School of Design with a degree in Fashion Design, but illustration is her first love. Raised in New Jersey, she now resides in Manhattan, where she works as a freelance illustrator. When not otherwise employed, Elizabeth spends her time contemplating theoretical physics, designing improbable apparel, and trying to remember to update her website, elizabeth-dran.net. 1987 HOSPITALIA, 1992 BONSAI DRESS (LLBD), 2002 BERTRAND DESPAIR GLOVE, 2005 HOOD-OLO

ANDRAÉ GONZALO feels that fashion is not just what you wear because it's cold outside—it's the mysterious alchemy that occurs if the world notices what you've chosen to wear, "because it is cold outside." A graduate of Otis College of Art and Design, he currently works as a freelance illustrator and "mercenary foot-soldier" in the battle for original American Fashion. He is distinguished for being a participant on Bravo's *Project Runway,* and a faculty member of FIDM in L.A. Speaking at colleges throughout the U.S., he lectures on Creative Design, as well as on how to determine "the new black" in five easy steps. 1927 ICE BEADING, 1950 FRIGIDAIRE FORMALS, 1953 POLY-CHEM OXFORD, 1957 FOUR O'CLOCK DRESS

AMELIA HAVILAND spent two years in the North Carolina School of the Arts high school visuals arts program, and went on to attend Rhode Island School of Design where she graduated with a BA in Film, Animation, and Video. Her work can be viewed online at http://theenchantedsnoconestand. weebly.com. **1903** SIDESADDLE MOTORING COAT, **1935** SAFARI PAJAMAS, **1995** ADIDIDAS

ANNIE LIM created her own collection, Mileinna, a vintage-inspired, easy-to-wear clothing line that's flirty, fun, and still comfortable, much like her personal design philosophy. She loves to create all different forms of art, be it fashion or illustration. She lives in New York and hopes to make a career out of making art. Contact her at anniej.lim@gmail.com. **1968** BEIGE LAMÉ, **1978** MACH2 LINGERIE

LILY NG graduated from Otis College of Art and Design in Los Angeles with a BFA in Fashion Design. While attending Otis, she mentored with Bob Mackie, Eduardo Lucero and Rod Beattie for LaBlanca Swimwear. She currently resides in L.A. where she works at a comtemporary fashion company and freelances as an illustrator. Contact her at lilyng204@yahoo.com. **1948** HAVANA OYSTER DIGGERS, **1985** FUSCHETTE, **1985** GILDED PINSTRIPES

ALISON PETRIE was born in Toronto, Ontario and has a degree in Visual Arts from the University of Western Ontario. In 2007, she completed a fashion design degree at Parson's School of Design in New York City. While attending Parson's, she interned with talented designers including Michael Kors, Inc., Proenza Schouler, Pink Tartan, and Arthur Mendonca. Her paintings have been commissioned by Lululemon Athletica. **1943** FIDELITY CARDIGAN, **1996** TRIFLING COAT

ISABELLA SCOTTO is influenced by many different styles especially those of the sophisticated twenties and thirties. Her elegant forms, geometric shapes and tall, slender figures are inspired by the Art Deco costume designs and stage sets of artist and designer Erte, with whom she shares a birthday. She works as a freelance fashion illustrator in Southern California. Contact her at isabellascotto@earthlink.net. **1910** PACING TROUSER, **1928** BERLIN BLACK